# Memoir of a 2G

Story of Secrecy and Resilience

# Memoir of a 2G

## Story of Secrecy and Resilience

Patricia C. Bischof

All rights reserved. No part of this publication may be reproduced, distributed, or transmitted in any form or by any means, including photocopying, recording, or other electronic or mechanical methods, without the prior written permission of the publisher, except in the case of brief quotations embodied in critical reviews and certain other noncommercial uses permitted by copyright law.

Copyright © 2019 Patricia C Bischof
All rights reserved
ISBN: 13-978-1721676804

*Dedicated to Henry and Ruth*

# CONTENTS

INTRODUCTION - 1
MY PARENTS COME TO AMERICA - 5
THE HOLOCAUST - 9
RELIGION - 19
MOTHER - 21
FATHER - 47
PARENTS - 63
GRANDPARENTS - 75

MY STORY - 77
My Youth - 79
My Mother and I - 85
My Father and I - 97
Faith - 101
Goals - 105
City Living - 111
School - 119
Employment - 131
College - 137
Leaving Home - 141
Love - 145
Travel - 149
Art - 151
Fear - 155
New York City - 161
Southwest - 165
Philosophy - 169

SUMMARY - 175
APPENDIX - 179
ACKNOWLEDGMENTS - 199
ABOUT THE AUTHOR - 201

# INTRODUCTION

If ever my close friends had said that someday I would write a book about myself, I would have rejected that vision. My writing a memoir would have been a total fantasy. An account of one's life is for the rich and famous, is it not? As a youth and an adult whose name was usually not in the limelight, I was just another ordinary person living an ordinary existence, or so I thought. What would have been so noteworthy about my life that I would want to set it down on paper, or for that matter why would anyone want to read about all my life's experiences? As I was searching my family history and genealogy, there were some memorable incidents I started writing about, stories that I thought were unique to my family and me. But don't unique life occurrences happen to just about anyone?

Connections create a togetherness of peace, cohesiveness, a relief, a pact of security. Tribes and groups go back centuries. Governments, barn raisings, dancing were constructed within a group emphasis of getting together for enjoyment and peace. As I was searching and searching for answers, I was wondering and hoping for answers and connections to my family that were either not talked about or that were totally elusive to me as a child growing up as well as now. We all need connections to our past and what has occurred to bring us into the present.

You will be reading about a story of how two people arriving in a new world were able to form a fresh home for themselves while bringing up a family of four children. It is also about how their history impacted me as one of these children. I believe my story needs to be told.

On some matters throughout my genealogical research, I did not have enough suitable information and had to fill in the blank spaces the best way I could for this book. My father and mother did not share information at all and questions that I posed to them most often were unanswered. They just did not want to talk about their past lives, period. As a youth and certainly as an adult, not knowing my family's background history, created a void in my life. Their silence left me with an abundance of unanswered questions, even to this day. For them and myself as a second generation, I want to be the voice to relate our stories as well and as accurately as I can with what minimal information that I have been able to obtain throughout the course of investigating my genealogy.

As a Second Generation or 2G woman, my experiences might be of some interest to people who have gone through a similar experience. For those who are not, perhaps this will help them understand and learn what it is like being brought up in this type of environment, by parents who came to this country without any kind of decompression groups, therapy or psychological help. It is an identifying term of someone whose parents endured, witnessed, and were involved during the Holocaust in the Second World War. In this book I will continue to use the term 2G.

I had no idea about the concept while I was growing up, that someone coming from my type of background might have some challenges. It has been a common experience that whenever I tried to explain in a group or with a person one on one, that my dad was in a concentration camp, or that I was a 2G, some people would exhibit an obvious strange reaction. Many times people would want to walk away from me or share on another topic for discussion; and classically, most often they would not want to ask any questions. They wanted to talk about anything frivolous and discount what I initially shared. There would be a void, a distance in the air, and a pause of not wanting to continue the conversation. It was a peculiar sensation and situation to be in. I felt that I was unable to be heard and there would be no further dialogue on the subject, period. Their discomfort might have stemmed from their lack of knowledge of this kind of history, or they had someone in their family who took part possibly, or that just maybe there might be some prejudice.

While growing up there were enough occasions where I felt and acted differently from my peers in school. In my youth and early adulthood, it was normal for me in school and social situations to feel rather inadequate. In school I was dressed much differently from my peers, and I felt somewhat European because of the different ways my parents brought me up. I was rather shy and silent. When I was young, I was unable to understand why I would feel this way. Of course I would feel or act this way! My father and mother were not born in America, hailed from two different parts of Germany, and brought with them their cultural experiences. It makes sense to me now.

So how am I to tell such a story? The best way that I know and remember! I would like to communicate with you what happened to my parents when they were young or that my mother did this when she was a child or that my father achieved that before arriving in America. All those types of topics can sound so simple and forthright. The fact is I am unable to answer what has eluded me for so long a time because I knew so little what occurred with either one of them before their arrival in the United States of America. *Nothing!* They did not share with me what their past lives encompassed.

I have changed some names to protect and respect privacy in the vignettes in this book. The stories are true as I saw them and as I have been able to as an adult to perceive, understand and resurrect them. There are some cases where I have had little of information on the topic being written about but found it profound and relevant enough to write about. That is also visible as these writings continue.

Writing about and acknowledging what happened to my parents is a way of giving them a voice. I am grateful to have the chance of giving them a mark of their existence under the adverse conditions that they endured. I am interested in telling how the destruction that impacted the lives of these two people also affected me, as well as the rest of my family. As miracles can and do happen, these two persons were able to enter the United States. This is a story encompassing heroism, strength, persistence, fear and hope.

## MY PARENTS COME TO AMERICA

The Second World War shook up the lives of everyone in Europe, obliterated and displaced millions of people. Out of that history came two refugees who landed in a new and foreign place, the United States of America. Neither one knew the other before coming to America. Even though they came from two different areas in Germany, they met after arriving in the world of golden opportunity. They were able to make a fresh start for an improved life in the States. Their names were Henry, my father, and Ruth, my mother. These two people were able to adapt themselves to a totally foreign surrounding and a new way of living, coping and acclimating to this transformed and strange way of life. Their lives were turned around before they arrived, as well as after living in the land of plenty, America.

My parents were unable to properly parent and explain to me what occurred in their past; this has left me clueless about what happened to them and my relatives in Germany and Poland. Much, if not most, of my generational history was lost, wiped out, and never talked about, ever. In most cases, children, as they grow up, learn about their extended family background from their parents, such as the telling of funny family stories, secrets, happenings, achievements and tragedies that were usually handed down through generations. That was absolutely not the case for me. Because my parents were unwilling to give me accurate, or for that matter, any information of what happened to my extended family, I was affected unfavorably.

Neither of them ever, ever talked about their lives in Europe. Nothing, and I mean nothing, was ever talked about- mum was the word! It was as if there were a shroud placed over their past. Mum was the word, and when I did pose questions as a youth or a young adult, my mother's scenarios went something like this, "Now is not the time." Not being able to tell her at those times how disappointed or upset I was, that she would react in that way by not talking at all, left a complete void of communication and a lack of understanding. I did not have the nerve or know how to express myself properly, and so I never got the answers to the many questions I still have yet today. Never did it come to be the proper time! And time was running out. And time did run out! By the time I felt able to converse with my mother, she had already died

As a child what does one know or expect of life? A child's upbringing is supposed to be filled with comfort, unparalleled love, attention, patience and learning. Perhaps this is only written on the white pages of the psychology books or in the fairy tales that I had been accustomed to reading!

It was not unusual for refugees entering the United States to have their surnames changed. Such was the case with my father. His surname was shortened from Bischofsheimer to Bischof, whereas my mother's surname stayed the same. Clerks taking down such unusual and lengthy last names spelled them the best way they could. Their responsibilities also included tallying up this immigrant population that entered into the United States in the late nineteen thirties.

While my parents were learning new skills, absorbing and surviving new ways to deal with life while living in America, they were bringing up a family. They had to acculturate into a new way of living. As they were educating themselves with this new way of living, I was brought up with the best possible intentions.

Memoir of a 2G

# THE HOLOCAUST

I am the first-born of four children; the first one born in the postwar generation in the United States of America, five years after my father was released from Dachau. In the past, I did not give much thought being the first born until I wanted to gain more information and history about my genealogy. One of my siblings said to me more than once, "You always speak about the Holocaust." And I said, "No! I do not always speak about the Holocaust, but I do speak about the Holocaust in that it is relevant to my story." That our parents survived the Holocaust and were able to go on with their lives is a miracle. The former history and life my father and mother experienced have had a major impact on me and for that matter on our whole family and certainly on all of us children. I will proceed to explain.

For some time I was unable to speak about or even admit much about my past. I was ashamed and confused about the way my parents brought me up, and did not want most people to know what happened to my family or for that matter what was happening within my family. Too, I was ashamed of being Jewish. Words and phrases that I would hear growing up were, "They are survivors," "They come from the old country," They lost everything," Holocaust survivors," etc. I had no idea what people were talking about and there was never a discussion as to what these statements meant. I just took this phraseology in and lived my life, with no explanations. Not until later on in my life did these terms and phrases have any meaning.

There were periods in my life when, if someone asked me if I were Italian, Spanish or Greek, I would answer, "yes." Nothing more needed to be said. I have an olive Mediterranean complexion with dark brown hair, and I could fit into any one of those ethnic groups. I did not want to admit the truth because of where I came from. I was uncomfortable and self-conscious about my culture. I wanted to fit in, be, look and act like all the other youth around me in school.

Now I appreciate my attributes, uniqueness and why I may be different, and what my background encompasses. I attempt not to compare myself to others. Sometimes that is not an easy task. Now, finally, I can accept the way and who I am, which is a miracle. I am proud of my family history and admire how my father and mother were able to adjust themselves to their absolutely new way of life.

I was not allowed to ask questions nor did I get answers to questions that I was brave enough to ask, and I felt confused with being different from my schoolmates. I had an incredibly strict upbringing; to question authority or to just ask simple everyday questions was *"verboten."* Mother's directives were to be immediately addressed and nothing else mattered at that moment. Rules were put into place; they needed to be abided to or else. I never gave the slightest inkling to go, do or think otherwise. My father was not the disciplinarian; he kept silent most times, whereas my mother gave the orders.

My mother often said, "Go to your room," and also, "Go clean your room." Backtalk was never an option for me, ever. She would say, "Don't give me any song and dance, just do it." When I was told to do something, I had better do it promptly. I had the cleanest bedroom in the United States, east of the Mississippi River!

I yearned to fit in, to have the skills and the popularity to be accepted by my peer group. What did I know! While I attended grade school in Nassau, New York, my upbringing was different and unique; I was unlike anyone in my class. Most times I kept silent except when I took care of my siblings. Even then, I was calm. One example stands out that was an unusual experience. After attending a Girl Scout meeting, I went to a girlfriend's home to wait for my father to pick me up after he arrived from work. When I went into her bedroom, on the walls were all these posters of Elvis Presley and names of popular singers I did not know. It was an unusual experience, as I was never allowed to listen to such popular music. I remember being in awe of all these Hollywood faces, with their bouffant hair, makeup and clothing style that was so foreign to me.

~*~

The Holocaust started on January 30, 1933 and Dachau Concentration Camp, the first concentration camp that was established, was first used for forced labor. It was located at an abandoned weapons factory area, which opened on March 22 of that year. As one enters the camp, a sign at the gate with the famous saying says, "*Arbeit macht frei,*" or "Work will make you free." Dachau is approximately ten miles northwest of Munich, the city where my father grew up and was born.

The Germans during the Holocaust kept scrupulous and accurate records that were saved, but were not until now accessible to the general public. This information is now available for anyone to search. These records have extensive and useful information about the incarcerations of victims who were held against their will in concentration camps and of those who were murdered. This information gives credibility to the atrocities and truths of what went on during that time. Answers to many unanswered questions can be found not only for me but also for many other survivors and children of survivors that until now have been kept secret from the public. One just has to have the fortitude to do the research and explore, write letters, and have the patience to wait for a reply and hopefully get responses. The United States Holocaust Memorial Museum, American Red Cross, Yad Vashem, and Center for Jewish History in New York City were exceptionally helpful in my research. Since the rise of the Internet, there are many places online to research one's family history.

The liberation of Dachau was on April 29, 1945 by the 42$^{nd}$ division of the United States' 7$^{th}$ Army. On May 8, 1945 Germany finally surrendered, and whoever was alive or barely alive was freed from the atrocities that they endured during the war.

The instincts for survival by individuals existing in Dachau had to be heightened, otherwise at any time one could be the next to succumb to physical or emotional abuse or death. One does what one has to do to survive. Whatever it takes, it is a stepping-stone towards the next level for one's survival. Towards the end of the war, Dachau was a most horrible place to encounter, and its dealings earlier were not that of a pastoral place of serenity; that was for sure. My father arrived at Dachau at the young age of 23 in August of 1935 and after twenty-two months of incarceration at the age of 25 on May 1937, he was finally released. For a long time, I wanted to know how he got out, and I am still amazed that he was even set free.

~*~

With a great deal of patience, I have been able to resolve a few questions I have had, although there are still a number of empty spaces. Somewhere down the line I heard from time to time discussions that my family had, but not specifically on how my father got out. What happened to him was just not talked about, period. I have been able to piece together a few bits and pieces of information on how he was able to get out of Dachau. His sister (who had already arrived in the United States) had most likely been able to sponsor him and pay for his release. Refugees who wanted to enter into the United States had to have a sponsor. She supposedly had some connection with someone higher up in the German military and was able to come to some agreement to set him free.

Living conditions in a camp were abominable; it is a miracle that he endured the length of time that he was incarcerated. It is a wonder that he even got released. Money can buy almost anything, especially one's life. In most cases, once people were incarcerated in a concentration camp, it was only a matter of time until they died. From Dachau, he finally arrived in the United States in July of 1937 to start a new way of life all over again. It is a miracle that he even landed in the United States, because the United States had restricted immigration from Europe, mainly Jews.

~*~

As a boy, my father attended a public school for five years and then graduated after six years of higher-level school. He went on to enter the business world, where he apprenticed for two years in the sales field, as a clerk. He worked for Max Ries & Company in 1935 until he was arrested in August of that year and sent to Dachau. I have been unable to find out anything about this company.

As an adult, his demeanor was subdued, nervous, and he was sad. He suffered a brutal arrest, had his nose broken, was days standing in water, experienced a bitter life and suffered extreme bodily punishment. He suffered from painful and dreadful varicose veins until his early death. The almost two years of internment in Dachau Prison were then followed by a government requested departure from Germany. My father's experiences certainly had an adverse affect upon him and changed his life forever. The mishandling of my father in Dachau created severe impairment of his health for the remaining years of his short life; he died at fifty. He was unable to achieve a workable proper income from his business and was never able to get back the tangible objects or monetary reparations for everything confiscated from him during the war. My father sought help going to a psychiatrist and psychologist for many years besides having the varied problems he encountered with his health.

~*~

This era brought about major changes to many individuals' lives, whether people were Jews or non-Jews, that is if these people were fortunate enough to live through those atrocious times. Most prisoners of war had gone through an ordeal living through rather horrific and brutal events and they wanted to forget about their human trauma they experienced. My parents most likely did not want us to be aware of such atrocities, and therefore never discussed what happened to them and the extended family.

Unlike today, in those times displaced persons and persons experiencing trauma did not have the luxury to attend group therapy, have counselors to talk to, medications, or the opportunity to attend decompression groups. Many survivors, once they were released from concentration camps and came over to the United States or traveled elsewhere, carried with them their horrific experiences. They had no one to speak to about what happened to them or others or what they saw and encountered. Quite often they would try to forget what happened. But by doing so they exhibited anger, were in some form of denial, or eventually involved themselves with addictions to help themselves cope with their entire trauma that they experienced.

~*~

Bringing up and taking care of four children is not an easy task for any parent under any everyday circumstance, but my parents especially had some challenges owing to their history. Definitely times were difficult for them while rearing us. While growing up I was an inquisitive child, asked a multitude of questions and as an adult I still do. My mother would usually tell me, "Not now." On her watch now was never the right time. When the time is appropriate, a mother may want to share with her daughter about her first kiss or about courting the man she finally married, my father, or what her relationship with her mother was like. These and so many other scenarios about what went on in my mother's life I have often pondered, were never discussed with me or shared by my mother.

~*~

The Holocaust destroyed most of my extended family on my father's side as well as that on my mother's side. About my mother's side I know almost nil. Due to the Holocaust, I was brought up without an extended family. Most of my classmates, friends and acquaintances had experienced and lived with the knowledge of their family history. I felt an abyss of not having an extended family, especially when I understood that many families had aunts, uncles, and grandparents, words that were rather foreign to me.

To this day, I have difficulty understanding the relationship of, let's say, cousins or uncles, because of my experience of not having them. I would hear of joyful stories and experiences told by my peers that included relatives, something that I could not even wrap my head around. Often when kids spoke about their grandparents or cousins, I would become confused, jealous and wondered why I could not relate. I did not have the opportunity to enjoy similar experiences. How could I? My relatives perished by being exterminated in the Death Camps. So, having the understanding of an extended family was an experience I was unable to attain. Many times I would hear these stories that would make my mouth water! "My grandfather just bought me a brand new bike," a young girl said to me. "I'm going to play with my cousins," this kid said to me. I had no understanding of these sorts of experiences, and I wanted all those good stories to happen to me too, that were happening to other children all around me. I wondered what it felt like to have grandparents. I would imagine happy occasions that the kids would talk about how grandparents could spoil their grandchildren, be their allies, and give gifts to them.

In the place of having an extended family, there were three special families that took the place of my grandparents. These older friends were kind, good cooks, loved me and showered me occasionally with gifts. Still, it was not the same as having an actual blood relative; blood relatives are blood relatives! The idea of experiencing a grandmother's or grandfather's love and nurturing would have been a welcomed addition in my life.

Memoir of a 2G

# RELIGION

I was brought up in the Jewish religion but in moderation. Even though my father was an agnostic, so I was told, my mother did have all of our family celebrate the major Jewish holidays. It is customary in the Jewish religion that the mother or older female figure of the family embrace the ceremonial obligations in the home like cooking and putting together a beautiful dinner table. My family lived in the country, Bunker Hill, New York, a very small area outside of Nassau, New York. On a few Sunday mornings, when I was in the third grade, I was picked up at a friend's home in another town and then brought to Temple Beth Emeth in Albany. This gave me the opportunity to learn the Jewish religion by attending religious school.

Religion was not a major focal point in my upbringing. But once I moved to the city with my family, I continued to attend temple. What the religious teacher discussed I cared less about, felt bored and lost, and in most cases did not understand what was being taught. Some of my peers felt the same way while others enjoyed it. But I did get confirmed and being a bit scared had to stand up in front of the congregation and recite a part of the Bible. A part of me felt as though I eventually learned and achieved something and that maybe this was a kind of life passage that I was supposed to go through. There were so few occasions when I would be the center of attention and by being involved in a ceremony such as this one in which my whole family would be attending, I felt self-conscious, but in a good way. This was a big deal and an important stage in my life. Never wanting to embarrass my parents or siblings was a concern I had. To toe the line and never cause any uncomfortable situation that would draw attention to my family or me was important, and I also feared repercussions from my mother should I have done something wrong or make her spew some nasty words. This passage of my life was over. I did well and made no mistakes, proud and pleased of the outcome and felt that I accomplished something worthwhile.

# MOTHER

While writing, I had so very little information and understanding about the plight of my parents. Enclosed, as an Appendix, is my mother's interview, with the USC Shoah Foundation Institute for Visual History and Education, that tells her story. I have been able to watch my mother's interview only two times, because it was too difficult. The third time, and only recently, I transcribed every word. When I started writing many years ago, I did not have some of the knowledge that I have now. There are stories about my parents that I have been unable to understand until now.

~*~

My mother was born on June 17, 1910 in the Prussian Empire, a part of Germany and a state that was German at the time, which makes her German. She became Polish in the year 1918, and in 1919, Eastern Prussia became a Polish state. In 1939 Poland got demolished. The area kept on changing from German to Polish and back. Tensions were getting high when my mother left. She was educated in Poland and then she left for the United States in 1937. She spoke little if ever of her challenges during this time of her life. It was as though she wanted to obliterate any thoughts from her mind pertaining to where she originally came from, and she did not want to remember or talk about what she previously went through even before the war. In WWII, Hitler attempted to turn this part of Poland into a German area, but did not succeed and the area is Polish to this day. I have a deeper understanding today as to the disinterest my mother had in Germany.

Not until I left home in my early teens to attend Girl Scout camp in the summers was I aware of my parents' accents. When I arrived home, I realized my parents' voices sounded different or peculiar compared to other people who I was accustomed to hearing while at camp. There was just enough difference in how their words were pronounced for me to notice.

~*~

My mother was a physically beautiful looking woman with long slender legs, smooth olive skin, hazel colored eyes, and dark brown hair that she wore in pigtails or coiffed in curls. She was five feet, nine inches tall. During the day, at times, she would wear a babushka tied over her hair set in curlers. It was a rare occasion that I saw her making any to-do about her beauty. She wore no makeup as far as I could see, other than lipstick, no nail polish, and dressed comfortably and conservatively, even wearing sneakers often. She was ahead of her time in that department, not as it is today somewhat the norm to see many women in business attire wearing running shoes to go to work in. She displayed much vitality, and enthusiasm for life and had many hobbies and interests such as sewing, gardening, reading, collecting cookbooks, and weaving. As she aged she never did look her chronological age, nor did she slow down accomplishing her activities.

~*~

My mother went to a German prep school from 1924-1927 in Posen, (Poznan) which was east of Neutimischel, the area where she was from and then went on to a woman's school seminary in Breslau (Wroclaw). She did the *Abitur*, which is a college prep exam, allowing her to study at the university. She then received her high school degree and was certified to become a teacher. Having been a daughter of a merchant who owned a general store, whose family sold hops to breweries and who belonged to the Jewish minority, this essentially made her middle class. Her family's interest in education indicated their upward mobility. She might have been encouraged to get educated, thereby attending University of Breslau, a teachers' college. This essentially gave her a feeling of superiority. Women were usually home bound if they came from a lower class. A teacher's college was more apt to be open to women, and she was on course to become a teacher.

~*~

My mother was well versed in many languages. She spoke German, Polish, Spanish, Hebrew and of course English. Her knowledge of the English language was impeccable. It was imperative that we children speak correctly. None of us kids were allowed to speak with any slang words, and I was reprimanded if I spoke improperly. While I was growing up, being lectured on how to speak had its disadvantages, but that type of upbringing has had its rewards for me today; I like to converse correctly and usually without the use of much slang.

She never allowed me to use a pronoun when referring to a person. A proper name had to be used and I could not say she or he! In referring to someone, I can still hear her say, "Don't say she, she is in the stable and says moo." It is somewhat awkward when I hear someone refer to someone by she or he. I find it strange but certainly have gotten used to that way of speaking.

~*~

My mother's experience was enormously different from that of my father, but a miracle just the same. She was able to leave her country and land eventually in the United States of America. But her life, like my father's, was disrupted and broken up; she had to start all over again. She sacrificed a lot in her life and worked hard.

In 1937, her mother placed her on a Polish medium size ocean liner, the M/S Pilsudski, which carried just fewer than six hundred passengers, and took approximately ten days to cross the ocean from Europe. Port of departure was from Gdynia, Poland and she traveled by herself sans any family members or friends to accompany her and was supposed to arrive in an unfamiliar place, the United States. That she came by Tourist Class indicates that she may have been financially well off and her name on The List of Passengers' manifest that I obtained has the word "Miss" before her name. There were few other passengers with the word "Miss" in front of their names. Out of the one hundred and fifty passengers in Tourist Class alone, she was one of only twenty-three single women. Most were married or couples and there was one Reverend. That she was in this environment, all alone, having no other relative or friend at her side had to be terrifying.

My mother never did get the occasion to see her mother or any of her immediate family and friends ever again. There is no question that her fortitude kept her going. To survive, she had to be strong, hide her feelings and get to her final destination, America. She had no idea what would be ahead of her in terms of conflict; she continued her trip across the ocean. Imagine a woman on an ocean liner all by herself, not knowing her destination, stopping first in Halifax, then eventually entering into the United States and then going to Cuba, then back to the United States, sounds overwhelming to me. My mother lived in Cuba waiting for her visa to get approved, and finally arrived for good into the United States in 1938. She never revealed anything about her happiness or unhappiness while she lived in Havana in 1937.

The year 1937 was a crucial year. It was the period when the United States put restrictions on the immigration process of people coming from Europe, especially Jewish individuals who were attempting to escape the turmoil in Europe. They wanted to seek refuge in the United States- a world of liberty, safety, and peace. Some European refugees who arrived from Europe landed in Havana, Cuba, but not after first living in the United States for a short while.

My mother's exposure to, and influence by, Cuba was shown by the scrumptious foods she made after arriving in the United States. Growing up in our home, our meals were made with a Cuban flair. Foods such as vanilla tapioca pudding, risotto, salmon patties, chicken gumbo, chicken fricassee, fried chicken wings, Spanish rice, cinnamon toast, and okra in soups were staples. These dishes were delicious especially the chicken gumbo with okra in it. My mouth is watering as I write. It is evident my mother did not eat this sort of fare while living in Germany. What Jewish, Polish/German, American person would have had these foods as their customary everyday cuisine? Eating these foods did not seem out of the ordinary at the time. I felt it was as common as drinking milk and consuming the ubiquitous American apple pie.

Only recently have I realized what a welcome addition my mother's experience in Cuba has been to my German and Polish heritage. She also played musical instruments such as castanets and maracas, instruments that were and still are popular in Latin American culture.

My mother tells her own story in the Appendix on page 179.

~*~

She was rather assertive, motivated, and outspoken at times in her relations with others and not at all quiet and reserved like my father. She attended a prep school in Germany that emphasized classical education, and prepared her for university. *Gymnasium*, a high school, prepares students for college, and its principles are that a student must study meticulously. When she arrived in America, she had already attained a college education in Germany, and in the United States she continued with her education by working towards her Master's degree in Education. Teaching different subjects in school, she became a physical education teacher and then became a popular kindergarten teacher in a public school, by incorporating the Montessori Method in her kindergarten classroom. Toward the end of her retirement, after teaching for ten years at Forest Park Elementary School of the South Colonie Central Schools, in Colonie, New York, from 1962 to 1972, she was honored with the Teacher of the Year award, which was quite a memorable occasion. The ceremony was held at the Northway Inn on February 3, 1972, in the evening, which included a dinner, and my mother received her award plaque from Mr. Washburn, her principal.

~*~

My mother was extremely talented. She captivated audiences with her beautiful soprano voice while singing Handel's *Messiah* with the Octavos singers in 1986. She also was an excellent baker and knowledgeable cook. She, as well, sewed extravagantly making gowns and men's suits. My mother was a terrific gardener, calculating where every seed should be planted. Too, she was an avid reader, getting a huge number of books from the local library.

My mother volunteered in the Neither-Nor Home Bureau, providing home and community services for women, became a leader in the Girl Scouts, and took part in other organizations. I have been unable to find out any specific information regarding mother's work at the Home Bureau but was able to read some newspaper clippings.

Helping others was an important value of hers, and she brought me up not only to help others, but also to give back to the community, and to take care of the environment, all of which have become an essential part of my life today. I volunteered as a Junior Girl Scout leader in Albany, New York. I checked wristbands on patrons getting into a dance venue at Lincoln Center, New York City, and I presently look after a bike and walk path in Tucson, Arizona.

For these values that she taught me, I am thankful. My mother's ability to take care of her family, hold a full time job and volunteer illustrate the energy that she had, considering the difficult life she had undergone during the war and when finally arriving in America. That my mother was able to teach me to help and care for others despite all the difficulties she endured, says much about her principles and character as a person, even though she was a tough and serious woman who meant business.

~*~

My mother was an avid reader and spoke English exceedingly well and correctly. While growing up in the country, she took out a subscription to the Book of the Month Club, selecting from their list of books that were available to each member, receiving a book or two once a month by mail. This gave her the opportunity to read, because where we lived was far from any library and my mother did not drive.

With her respect for books, she would say often to me, "Do not write in or dog-ear the pages in that book." So that rule has been so ingrained in me, that when I went to college, I found it difficult to write in my books. I did it anyway, yet minimally.

~*~

My mother did not imitate others, had her own mind and ran to the beat of her own drum. Conformity was not one of her attributes or virtues! She did not appreciate fads and did not care what the fashion industry dictated. If it looked good then wear it, but if the fashion industry, magazines or TV said such and such, she could not care less. The hairstyle for gals in the fifties was a bouffant filled with loads of hair spray. That did not enter into my mother's mindset whatsoever. Being genuine and original were important components in her life that she instilled in me. To be true to oneself was an important virtue of hers. What others thought or said about her or her ideas made no impression on her.

~*~

Most often my mother was the one bringing home the larger salary and keeping our home financially stable. She did this by becoming the physical health director of a YWCA in Albany, New York. She taught physical fitness classes and was well respected; her classes were always filled with women who were interested in this new way of exercising and keeping fit, and a new way of learning how to take care of their bodies. Physicians referred women to these classes after their post surgical procedures or after giving birth to their babies. It was an innovative workout designed by Elizabeth Mensendieck called the Mensendieck System. My mother was ahead of her time in many respects. It was not the norm as it is today to be independent and for a woman to be the breadwinner. Jack LaLanne fitness centers and private health clubs and spas were not yet open and not as prevalent as they are today. She was progressive when it came to teaching and implementing women's workout and health programs.

Five years after my father's death, on August 20, 1968, my mother remarried and ended up with her second husband for thirty years.

~*~

A while ago, a close friend, Susan, told me that she had just viewed an early morning television program, on which Holocaust survivors were able to tell their stories by setting up an interview. She did not remember the name of the program, but there were only three key television early morning channels in my area: ABC, NBC and CBS. I was able to find and contact the TV station, and what transpired after that telephone conversation became a wonderful yet grueling, emotional experience for me.

In 1994, Steven Spielberg founded the USC Shoah Foundation Institute for Visual History and Education, originally called the Survivors of the Shoah Visual History Foundation, that provided an opportunity for a Holocaust survivor or a witness of that era to be interviewed and filmed by a two-person team. The foundation would send out two people to interview anyone willing to share what happened to them during WWII. I had an intuitive feeling that this would be a suitable opportunity for my mother to tell her story, even though she never spoke about what had happened to her.

By explaining to my mother what would be going on with the interview process and persuading her to do this interview would take some coaxing on my part, or so I thought. To my surprise, my mother, the one who told me so little and was so secretive, was willing to be interviewed. Wow! I was absolutely flabbergasted. To say that hearing her story was a pivotal moment for me was an understatement. I absolutely had no idea that it was going to be this simple. That she was interested in talking about her past was a total miracle. I believe that the credibility of the organization helped make this key move and it was also towards the latter part of her life. This was the only time, and I mean the ONLY time she ever opened up about herself, ever.

Two people would be going to my mother's home; one would interview her while the other would film the whole episode. I was asked to stay in an adjacent room so as not to distract my mother while she was interviewed. What they would be asking her beforehand I had absolutely no idea. All I knew was that they were interviewing people like her to document what went on in Europe during the Holocaust. In preparation for her interview, she had gotten some props together, such as an old doll from her youth, and some official papers and dated photographs from her past. With some trepidation I was looking forward to this because of what I might hear and learn. This was an incredibly big leap and a risk to open up to two complete strangers. Through this process perhaps I would finally hear some answers to some questions that I still had.

I felt fearful of what, for the first time, I would hear coming from my mother's lips. Finally willing to tell her story, she did it with astounding aplomb. She wanted this interview to tell the public the truth of what went on during this time in her life. While sitting in the adjoining room listening and at the same time writing down as rapidly as I could the information that was for the first time revealed to me was absolutely profound. It was heart wrenching. I remember crying, but keeping quiet as not to interfere with her process. Even though I was learning and hearing all this for the first time, it was so difficult to remember and comprehend. It was a long process and having to encapsulate all this new information in a few hours, for me, had some drawbacks. I was overwhelmed.

When the interview finally concluded, the interviewer asked me to come into the room with them and invited me to say anything I wished. My mother could see that I cried. I surmise that her discomfort and awkwardness of finally telling her story was evident by her stating, "I had to do these things," before I even said a word. Given her age and the emotional aspect of bringing up her past, I am sure she was physically and emotionally exhausted. This interview, I now understand, was a way for her to accomplish her healing in a safe environment and to let people know what the Nazis had done to demolish and totally change her life; it took away her life as she knew it.

~*~

My mother had fewer problems assimilating into the American way of living than my father. Even though my mother was educated when she arrived in America, she still had to start from the bottom up by establishing herself as a working woman in many menial capacities. At the beginning, she was an au pair, a governess, sold fruit drinks at a fast food restaurant called Orange Julius in New York City, and sewed gowns and suits privately for well to-do clients. She eventually got all her papers in order to teach in a public school.

~*~

The parents of one of my mother's students requested she teach all the siblings as they began kindergarten. That was how much my mother was admired and appreciated as a teacher. Although strict, she incorporated many values in her class. I visited her classroom and all her students stood up when I entered the room. This was one example of her type of instruction. Her popularity was due to her particular method of educating kindergarten children. She took her teaching seriously. She wanted children to listen to what she said and learn to follow directions. She took much interest in her students and even took up a collection of clothing for some of her kids who were financially strapped and lived in a trailer park. Once home, unwinding from a full day's work, she would get a bunch of grapes or cut up apple, put them on a white paper towel and take them to her bedroom. She would then sequester herself in her bedroom with the door closed for an hour or two.

~*~

During my growing up years, my mother would find fault with something that I created even though I was fairly artistic and creative. Making doll clothing from scraps of fabric found around the home and putting together something from paper was a usual way of occupying my time in my room. Her negative responses crushed me immensely. It saddened me and I always hoped just once she would give me some kudos but that never materialized. I have been perplexed by her method of disciplinary actions that was used on all of us children. She would also compare me with this one particular girl. Her assessment made me feel stymied. I felt awful that my mother would make this comparison. She was only aware of the girl being an accomplished student who brought home good grades.

~*~

One of my mother's realities was that I was supposed to accomplish everything with immediacy and accuracy. Foolishness and frivolity were to be eliminated at all costs. "If you want to be silly, I will give you something to be silly about," she said more than once! "Yes, this instant, I want everything to be picked up immediately," was another one of her mantras. I lived within a serious framework in our family, and I was not to take life at all lightly. Life had its challenges, and it did not matter that I was a child either. Tasks needed to be completed, and they were to be done perfectly. I was usually full of anxiety, bit my nails lots, and afraid that I would be reprimanded or that I would fail to achieve the expectations set upon me by my mother. Nothing was ever good or done well enough. My mother told me to dust the living room and after I was finished her reply was, "I thought you said that you dusted this living room!" And I said, "I did." My mother, who stood five feet and nine inches would run her hand across the top of the fireplace, a place I could never have reached as a child, and showed me an area where I missed. Rather young, I quickly learned not to fool around or make mistakes because of the repercussions that could possibly take place. I was only a child!

Seldom would I hear my mother apologize for anything. She thought she was always right; she liked to tell everyone what to do. Her boldness did not have any room for humility. While I was home one afternoon conversing with her over the telephone, she replied, "I'm sorry" to something that I had said. You would have thought she offered me the moon! I was so shocked that I asked her to repeat what I just heard. I asked, "What did you say, Mother?" and she repeated her apology again. To hear her humility and admission that she was wrong, never having heard that before from her, shocked me. It truly amazed me.

~*~

While I was growing up there was no room for frivolity and fun; seriousness and hard work were the rule. This attitude of my mother's aided her everlasting strength and resilience and is what empowered her to exist and endure in what would be her next big or small challenge to living.

~*~

Being patriotic and respectful towards the American flag and what it means to be an American were important virtues my mother bestowed upon me. In front of our country home was a flagpole with the United States flag. She was aware of the privileges and opportunities I had by being an American. When viewing a parade, if there were an American flag present, she would insist that I put my right hand over my heart and say the Pledge of Allegiance. It was compelling for her to be seriously American and to become acculturated into its lifestyle. That became apparent by her not wanting us children to know the German language, but to enunciate and speak English well, with absolutely no slang.

My mother's conversations with my father could pertain to our birthdays, just private talks, arguing, or anything else; I eventually became aware of this and ultimately picked up bits and pieces of the German language. I could not speak fluently but ended up taking German in high school. I recalled many German words that I heard from my mother and father.

~*~

Whenever my mother introduced my sister and me to someone, she would say that I was the beautiful daughter whereas my sister was the smart one. I was brought up to be unconcerned with my looks, but when she would say I was pretty to someone, I felt very uncomfortable. It hurt me that I could not be smart or my sister could not be pretty. I remember I would cringe when I heard her say this to people. I certainly yearned to be as smart as my sister and wanted to hear my mother say just once that my sister was pretty too. I felt I was stupid no matter how hard I tried. I would figure things out or come up with answers, but maybe not as fast as my mother would have liked. The fear of making an error was foremost in my mind. I wanted to work in harmony with my mother, to make her happy and be happy with me, but it all seemed so futile. She used to tell me that I was stupid. Later on in my early twenties, a fellow said that I was attractive and smart; I will never forget that statement, that a woman had the capacity to be good-looking and smart. I know today that the statement from my educated mother telling me I was beautiful but stupid had an adverse effect on me.

~*~

There was an incident when she was a senior citizen. There was a community center in Albany that my mother occasionally went to. They served free lunches. When she went there, they thought my mother was not a senior and that she was trying to get a free lunch. She looked that much younger than her years. My mother lived to the age of 86, and still did not look her chronological age. I knew incredibly little about her when she died, for that matter she knew little about me, a sad commentary!

~*~

When my mother found out that she was pregnant with my youngest sibling, it was rather a surprise to her. She was not a young woman; she was forty-four. After finding out she was pregnant, my mother went to my father's place of work to tell him the news, and he seemed to be in a state of shock. He probably was not up to having another child added to the three children they already had. My parents probably had not planned on having any more children, especially later on in life. I believe that they were not prepared monetarily and emotionally, and this perhaps created an even more stressful period in their lives. When my young brother came home from the hospital, I remember having the responsibility of taking care of him then and years after.

~*~

It was important to my mother that all of us children learn how to swim. We all attended Red Cross swimming lessons during the summer break from school. On Sundays in the summers, with my father driving, our whole family would pack into the car and head out to go swimming where there was a deep creek that was unpolluted. We ate a picnic lunch that mother put together. Lunch consisted of homemade German potato salad, sandwiches, and tomatoes from the garden, a welcome addition to our swimming in the late mornings. We had to wait one hour after eating before we were allowed back in to swim. This creek was crystal clear glistening water, so deep that it cast a cavernous dark charcoal color on its surface. At one side there was a tree with a thick frayed rope that kids would jump off of and land in the water. While we were waiting for our food to digest, my mother would have all of us children pick up trash left behind by other bathers and picnickers. As stated previously, we were taught early on as children not to litter and to respect the property we lived on. By late afternoon all of us were exhausted from the long day's event. We headed back home, having a forty-five minutes' drive ahead of us.

~*~

During hunting season, it could become scary where I lived. My home in the country was surrounded with one hundred acres of woods, meadows and swamps. Because of Eminent Domain, twenty acres had to be sold to a power company, putting all these massive power lines across twenty acres, leaving the rest of the eighty acres alone. Even though we had all these beautiful eighty acres, posted signs were never put up to keep hunters or anyone else off the property.

When hunting season came in the fall, hunters thought that it was open season for anyone to go on the property. They never came up to the door to ask if they could hunt, they just took the liberty to hunt on it. My mother would become furious when she heard and noticed a hunter. It probably stirred up much fear, especially because we wandered all over the land. With her German accent and her hair up in a babushka, she would scream at the top of her lungs for them to leave immediately. She would run out of the house, telling them off. It is a miracle nothing unpleasant happened to her or any of us, knowing we spent so much time wandering in the woods. It is remarkable that no one got hurt or killed.

~*~

On a few occasions my mother would tell some of her friends' fortunes using a regular deck of playing cards. There was an aura around this topic; nothing was ever discussed or explained to me. It seemed eerie. Where and how she learned to read cards, I have no idea. Did she learn in Germany or Cuba? A friend of hers would come over to my home to have her fortune told when my family and I were living in the country, and mother told us emphatically, "Go outside and play, and do not come back into the house until I tell you so." Under any circumstance, while my mother was telling someone's fortune, we stayed outside or else!

~*~

There was a woman who liked my mother a lot and enjoyed her company. At the time I was a teenager. She came over to our house and brought me a brand new beautiful deep turquoise, long sleeved shirt with white mother of pearl buttons. It was folded up nicely, and it looked like it came from an expensive store. It was rather unusual for me to have something brand new, especially something to wear. Our family never had the financial means to go out and purchase new cloths on a whim. The friend was using this way of showering me with gifts to impress and get close to my mother; I understand this now. What she did not know was that my mother could never be bought, had high principles and certainly would not have acquiesced to such a situation. No sooner did she arrive, and then she had to leave! That something did not go well, I could tell. I could not ask my mother what happened, because I knew what her response would be, "Never mind!"

My mother eventually explained to me that this woman liked her a lot. I figured out that this woman made a pass at my mother or said something to her that she did not approve of and my mother asked her immediately to leave. That this woman used me as an intermediary and she was making a kind gesture to me so that my mother would care about her had no impact on my mother. This was my first experience with adult sexuality in what constituted someone liking someone of the same sex, let alone that my mother was already married to my father. I was just a kid and it was difficult to understand the situation, since I only understood that a man and a woman could fall in love. That this woman liked my mother, nothing further was going to occur, that was evident.

~*~

Not only was my mother an accomplished weaver- having two Leclerc looms, one of which was forty-five or sixty inches in width, but also a terrific gardener, an outstanding cook and an exceptional baker. One of her rooms contained one thousand cookbooks she bought at garage sales over the years. From the kitchen ceiling would dangle various sizes and shapes of pots and pans she accumulated for her baking needs. Trying to find a better baker has been close to impossible even to this day. Not only were my mother's ingredients top notch, the quality and looks of her baking were second to none. People today still reminisce and talk about this gift. She utilized the metric system using gram scales. Some scrumptious examples of her baking consisted of lebkuchen, chocolate pretzels, honey cake and molasses creams. These were so mouthwatering the flavors created a dance upon our palettes.

~*~

There was one especially notable incident to one of my mother's type of cooking. One of my girlfriends came over for dinner and my mother had prepared tongue. When my girlfriend Pat saw the presentation of tongue placed on the serving plate and it was not cut up, she was repulsed. For those of you that have never experienced the taste, it is delicious. Mother's culinary gifts came from the fruits and vegetables from her garden, the freezer, and items she canned.

Most every bright-eyed American kid is brought up with peanut butter and knows what it is, right? Wrong! As a teenager, my mother and I were visiting family friends. Around lunchtime I was asked if I would like to have a peanut butter and jelly sandwich. I never heard of that before, and I went to my mother and asked her if I could have it. That was my first experience of having that especially American food. The sandwich, something that I was unaccustomed to eating, had a wonderful, strange, sweet smelling taste from the jelly and sated my palate.

~*~

What were particularly fun times for me were around birthdays when my siblings and I could pig out and devour a cake of our choosing that my mother baked from scratch. The wafting of sumptuous smells filled the whole house. The sad part was that I was not allowed around her in the kitchen when she was completing all these wonderful pieces of art. I was allowed back in the kitchen when all the baking was finished and then I had to wash every pot, pan, and utensil and clean up the kitchen. That I was not permitted in the kitchen when she cooked and baked saddens me. To partake in her knowledge of baking and cooking would have been enlightening. Of course, I finally learned how to cook on my own but not until much later. And I am not bad at it either!

~*~

My mother's idea of how food was to grow came from her gardening experience. She would till and develop wonderful gardens; she would know the Latin names of plants she grew at home and in the garden. We had a chicken coop that was home to many chickens and one rooster. The chicken eggs were freshly laid daily. Much of the food grew from the earth, and she made cakes that were something to drool over, her famous sponge and chocolate cakes, éclairs. My mother also made terrific 3-bean salad, and chicken fricassee. When I was growing up I never had store-bought-anything that I can remember. When she doled out food at dinnertime or lunchtime I had better finish what was on my plate or I would hear her mantra, "Eat and finish what's on your plate," telling me that, "There are starving children!" I was never allowed to go to the refrigerator to get food for myself, and I was conditioned never to eat between meals.

Snacks and junk food were not part of my food intake at home. In fact, I did not even know that there were all these wonderful foods called snacks or sweets. It wasn't until I would be at someone's home, that I found out.

My mother often said, "There are children dying in Biafra," and "If you want more, there are more potatoes." Biafra was a southeastern region of Nigeria, around the late nineteen sixties and early nineteen seventies, devastated by civil war and famine. The table was always set properly usually by one of us kids, and the guests were well content with the food that was served.

~*~

Close friends of my family would be invited to Passover Seders, Rosh Hashanah and Chanukah meals to share and experience these joyful festivities in my home. My mother would hold court. Her incredible cooking, with scents that wafted throughout the house was a welcome addition to any one of the holidays we celebrated. Her matzo ball soup was superior, and I have yet to encounter as good a soup anywhere else. Examples of her delectable holiday cooking and baking were her sponge cake with homemade whip cream with fresh luscious strawberries from the garden, potato pancakes, lamb, challah, and mashed potatoes. My experience of eating challah as good as the one she made has been rare. Hers was exceptionally light, sweet, and had a smooth texture and was baked having the top with whipped egg to give the surface a light brown golden glow. As long as it would take for her to make all these mouthwatering holiday foods, it would take all of us but a few moments to devour them. The table was always set with a starched white linen tablecloth, linen napkins, fine china, and flowers picked from our garden such as yellow forsythia. It was a sight to behold. My mother baked a delicious ham. This was unusual, because Jewish people usually do not eat pork, even though at the time I had no idea.

Memoir of a 2G

# FATHER

My father was born on April 5, 1912, and came from Munich, Germany. He lived there until he was forced to go to the Dachau Concentration Camp. He probably came from a family that was pretty well integrated into the middle class. My father, though a sophisticated man, had an attitude that came from his cultural background, a bit different from my mother's. My father loved the Germanic society; eating, drinking and the arts made him who he was. A pure German's emphasis on being German was of the utmost importance.

~*~

He was five feet, eight, very thin, weighed one hundred thirty eight pounds when he arrived in the United States. He had hazel eyes, a trimmed thin mustache, and his right index finger was deformed. In most of the photographs taken of him while here in the States, he usually held a cigarette in his one hand while he has a solemn look on his face. He dressed with a refined European flair, and his demeanor seemed calm and solemn. When one of our friend's husband, Lou, would be with him, my father's demeanor would change to a happy one. I was aware of that. My father seemed fond of Lou, felt comfortable with him, and Lou liked and respected my father deeply. My father seemed to be at ease and would smile which was especially unusual. My father would have discussions with Lou that he would not have with others.

~*~

My father was a refined and kind gentleman, rarely raised his voice and was usually calm. That my father's concentration camp experience had an effect upon him in later life is an understatement. As a child and adolescent, I often observed how serious and quiet he was, gazing out into space, and once I heard him singing a rhyme in German out loud that he learned in the camp. He may have been depressed. He did not like being in the United States and often complained about the American way of life. Most often what upset him was the wastefulness in this country or in our home. He would eat the stale bread in the bread bin. He typically was smoking an unfiltered cigarette and rarely speaking. His background did not convey a happy life. Having been put into a concentration camp at an early age definitely had an impact on his thoughts, feelings, and surely his behavior. I am sure he was deeply traumatized by his almost two years in Dachau where he suffered war trauma. His experiences probably ruined his health. When I was a young girl, I would kiss him good night. My mother would say, "Go give your father a kiss good night." There would be a scent from a cigarette or a pipe that he recently smoked and a slightly rough cheek that would have a shadow of a day's growth of a beard. I think he liked that I did that. I do not know, because he was a man of few words.

~*~

Before my father established his own retail textile fabric store, he worked for somebody else's company selling fabrics along with drapery while we were still residing in the country. Traveling to work by automobile took around forty minutes, not having the convenience of an expressway yet. When he came home from work he usually seemed exhausted. He was as I have already mentioned, a quiet man, just sitting, staring out into space and smoking his cigarette when he was home. He too would smoke at the store and anywhere else. Those were the times when there were no restrictions on smoking in public spaces, buildings and stores.

~*~

One example of my father's affection for Germany was his love of Wagner. That was a prime example of his sophistication. Though he endured much torture in Dachau, it did not lessen his love of opera and classical music, especially Richard Wagner, who was anti-Semitic. It is rather common for German Jews to be moderately relaxed about their Jewish religion. For my parents being German had much more significance than being Jewish, I believe. In my mother's case though, as an Eastern European Jew, she did not have that cultural love for Germany as much as did a pure German like my father.

Today I have a better and clearer understanding of my parent's attitude towards Germany; it was due to the areas they came from. As an example, it is somewhat analogous to having a person coming from a rural country area of Vermont marrying someone from the Deep South, let's say Savannah, Georgia. It makes more sense to me now as to the different cultural backgrounds each of my parents had, that they came from two opposite ends of the spectrum in ideals, religion, and culture. Talk about opposites attract! In the case of my father and mother, their interactions were like oil and water, argumentative and enough times hostile and uncommunicative.

~*~

While working on my genealogical research, I was able to track down and find out my father's Dachau Concentration Camp number. The Nazis used prisoner number 8048 to process him. He did not have this number for identification tattooed on his arm, as was the practice later on throughout The Holocaust. The tattoos were a numbering system for documentation and for keeping track of all of prisoners. He had entered Dachau in the beginning of incarcerating people; the forces had not started to use tattooing yet. Our family had a friend who did have his number tattooed on his arm and no one ever spoke about why he had or how he got this tattoo. It was like a shadow hovering over me. It was there but never acknowledged. I also did not understand why any person would have a number tattooed on his or her arm anyway. It just did not make any sense to me. And mum was the word as I was growing up, no explanation or discussion, period!

~*~

What I have wondered about most often was what my father did or did not do to get incarcerated in Dachau Concentration Camp. He was of the young age of twenty-two, and it must have been devastating for him to be there. I worked for twenty plus years searching for answers; recently, I finally got the reply. While sifting through a vast trove of documents retrieved from various places, I came upon one document, written in German, that helped me understand why he was sent, and there is no more wondering. I was able to find out that he was put into Dachau because he was a *Rassenschänder*, which is a German word that means race defiler. This German word has a varied and deep meaning in that it means race shame and that one could or would die because of this concept. The topic and idea are quite complex. Anyone having a relationship or friendship formed between an Aryan and non-Aryan was punishable by law, especially between Aryans and Jews, and if found out, a person could be or would be placed into a concentration camp, or put to death. As best as I can piece the facts together, I found out my father had a relationship with an Aryan woman. He was found out by the authorities and taken to Dachau. And for going out with an Aryan! The SS used any excuse of minor conduct or an infraction that they did not approve of to put someone away. Finally- I do now have an explanation. To imagine anyone being incarcerated there for even one hour, let alone almost two years, I cannot envision. I feel sad and angry that he had to succumb to suffering. My father's few years were taken away from him. He did not date, travel, go to college, experience hobbies or just his daily life, everyday living. I am angry that this political arena developed in such a grotesque way.

~*~

On another earlier form, different from the form above, I filled out all necessary spaces to get any type of information as to why my father was rounded up and taken to Dachau. The form came back from the German government. In the response that I received, that box was left blank. The German government had left that space blank! Again, the obvious answer is probably that he was a Jew.

My mother gave me the original official document from the German government from Dachau Concentration Camp showing my father's release with the actual dates, a swastika and even the commandant's name. This is a piece of evidence to show the reality of what happened to him and a miracle that he was even released. To have such information and see my father's name on many documents I was able to retrieve from my genealogy research gives me chills. Examining such accurate and relevant information doesn't make the story any easier, but it does verify what happened. So much has been and is written questioning if the Holocaust really did take place. It did.

Under the Nuremberg Laws, in 1935, Jews were incarcerated and when they were released, as my father was, they were not permitted to talk about what happened.

~*~

Imagine this scenario: you are standing around in a circle with friends your age. You are then told, not asked, with all the others around the circle, to stone the fellow standing in the center of the circle, until he is dead. Events such as this were a customary occurrence. This is just one example of what my father had to go through while imprisoned in Dachau. The commandant gave this order to your group and if not obeyed, you would most likely be the next in the circle. Living in this kind of anarchy is an incredibly stressful and scary sort of existence from day to day. Not knowing whether you were the next one to die certainly had to be a most stressful way to survive. I had heard some bits and pieces of this story a few times, but it was quite vague and it made little sense to me. Now I have a better understanding.

~*~

I located a certificate that enabled my father to immigrate to the United States. Because it was in German, I had it translated to English. It stated that my father was a tradesman, and that in the last five years he lived in Germany he was not judged for a crime. It also stated he was not a beggar, nor did he commit any crimes. Furthermore, there were no charges against my father at the time of the certificate. This official document was necessary for him to enter into the United States. He also lost his German citizenship after leaving Dachau. It is interesting that the Germans did not consider imprisonment in Dachau a crime. Amazing!! For the Germans to admit this would have meant the Germans early on would be acknowledging that they indeed did have camps. They did not want proof of such camps, least of all, on paper. They did not want the world to know yet. They were slick operators.

~*~

I would occasionally watch my father trim his beard when I was young. He trimmed his mustache by putting a stiff piece of paper next to the edge of his mustache so it would be even when he cut it. I loved watching him do this. When he met a lady, he would usually acknowledge her by taking off his hat and then putting it back on again, an old fashioned custom. An especially classy man, his manners were impeccable. The integrity with which he and my mother lived had an indelible impression on me. They seemed like classy adults.

~*~

I do not believe my father had a college education. When he came to this country by way of the Hamburg American Line, he worked as a salesman for others. He eventually opened his own retail textile store that was stocked with gorgeous fabrics that were used to make clothing, curtains and drapes. He had exquisite and elegant taste that showed especially when he purchased fine materials such as worsted woolens, brocades, silk shantung and silk cloths for his store. Few customers were interested in these and wanted much less quality fabrics with cheap prices. If someone wanted to have custom draperies or curtains made, they most likely shopped at my father's store; he had an excellent choice of fabrics. He was planning on moving to a larger store and having a much bigger inventory. He died at the young age of fifty, leaving my mother with the four of us children.

~*~

I will never forget the time when my father came home pretty excited about a brand new product that was coming out on the market, a new discovery. My father's enthusiasm was unusual; he usually was quiet and somber. He indicated how this was going to be a big deal and change the business climate in clothing, accessories, along with many other items. Boy, was he right! This new product was called Velcro, where two pieces of fabric were created that would stick together and yet could be pulled apart and then put back together again. A salesman came to the fabric store where he worked, showed everyone this new phenomenon. It was derived from an ordinary plant called burdock. Burdock sticks to everything it comes into contact with. This new idea of sticking two pieces of product together would be the next great invention. I was able to see this before anyone in the mainstream. And what an invention it was!

~*~

My father died unexpectedly. He showed no signs of being ill. It was a shock to me as well as to my mother and the rest of the family. I did not know how to react, because I had never gone through a death to someone close to me before. I had planned to finally sit down with my father eye to eye and talk intimately about what went on in his life before coming to America. I wanted to learn about his dreams, his passions, his parents, (my grandparents), and so on. This time of closeness with him was never allotted me; it was a big loss in my life. Not ever having had the time or occasion is like a shallow path through a forest of empty trees with no branches. No one ever knows his or her fate in life. And especially what his or her last day will be. He was returning home by bus from his full day at work, leaving his usual bus stop at the end of our street to venture home, when he had a heart attack. He never came out of it. I was told that the neighbors attempted to revive him, but he never responded to their help. I was working at the time in Albany and living at home; I was twenty-one.

~*~

When we all were returning from the cemetery, one of my girlfriends was at my house. She put a bucket of water at the front entrance to wash our hands; that is a custom in the Jewish religion. It is also a custom for Jews to bury the dead immediately after their death, everything happened so fast. This was my first experience regarding death, services and mourning. Friends came over to my home after the burial and brought all kinds of food. Even though he was quiet most often, this loss surely changed the mood and dynamics of my family. Just hours before he died, I spoke to him over the telephone while he was at his fabric store, and he was looking forward to continuing our conversation after he got home. It was at this juncture in our relationship that I was getting to know him better and was speaking to him more.

~*~

My father especially hated waste of any kind and it riled him to no end if we children left any of the lights on and not to squander was drilled into us. When leaving a room, he would ask, "Did you turn off the lights?" Leaving them on would cost money and be wasteful. Food was not to be thrown out, and he went absolutely bonkers if he found wasted food.

Behaviors common among survivors of the Holocaust were to be frugal, not waste food, no matter how small the pieces were, and keep a low profile. My father was no exception to this form of behavior. While in Dachau, a morsel of food could make the difference between living and dying, to err in the slightest meant death.

I particularly remember an incident when my father opened up the bread drawer we had in the kitchen. There were just a few bread ends in the back of the bin that had gotten a bit hard. We never heard the end of it. It was one of the few occasions when I saw him go over the edge by yelling at all of us. He went ballistic if I had to get something from the refrigerator, I could not leave the door open for any length of time. My mother was not as strict about wasting food as my father, and I attribute his outburst to something regarding his imprisonment. In fact, I am sure of it, of his experience he endured of not receiving adequate food and starving. Even today I am careful to not waste and can sometimes envision and hear his voice in the back of my head. He left an indelible impression on me about how important it was not to waste anything.

~*~

I remember an incident regarding my father while I was in the seventh or eighth grade and we were still living out in the county. I called my sister an inappropriate name. I swore! She went to Dad and told on me. After washing the dishes, I had retired to my bedroom with my door closed. My bedroom was lovely. It had white wallpaper with beautiful red roses and light green leaves on it. Hearing a knock on my door, I opened it, somewhat surprised, and in the hallway standing there was my father. This was unusual because he seldom came to my room. My sister had always been his pet, could do little wrong, and got away with things; that she was five and a half years younger than I was added fuel to this situation. He proceeded to ask me if I had called her a bad name. I said, "Yes!" He slapped me across the side of my face. Never before had I ever seen him raise his hand to us children; I was humiliated, scared and shocked. I found this to be over reacting and have always wondered if it had anything to do with his experience in the camp. Never have I attempted to call my sister or brothers any bad name ever again, I can assure you that! A good lesson learned!

~*~

At the dinner table there were some times when my mother would become incensed with my father. Her face turned red and her voice was shrill. She would insinuate something and yell something at him. This made no sense to me. On one such occasion, she blurted out, "You would do that for Miss Jones!" He had made the acquaintance of a woman who was fond of him, and my mother would throw this up in his face while all of us were sitting around the dinner table. This happened more than once; I can still remember some of those outbursts from my mother as if they were happening right at this moment. He uttered nothing. Whether he liked this person or not I have no idea, but the fact that my mother would be so angry and say this in front of us children while we were all together at the dinner table is astounding to me. I felt this strange feeling for him, that he was being denigrated in front of us. Eventually, it blew over.

~*~

An interest my father took up later in his life was painting landscapes in the outdoors called en plein air. He sat outside in the field behind our home with his easel, canvas and oil paints and paint beautifully. Sadly, he supposedly got rid of his paintings. I never did see any later on in my life. He could paint being surrounded by a serene and spectacular natural setting. It gave him a place to relax and be at peace, something that he was not too accustomed to doing. On a few occasions, I also sat and painted with him. There was one rare occasion that I can remember where he and I had a special moment together, even though we spoke infrequently, or I would say absolutely nothing at all. These meaningful times left me with much love because of these short intervals alone with him and having him to myself with no one else around. This was certainly an unusual instance for me in that I was able to just be me and not work or do my chores. I could be with him and that was an exceedingly rare and unusual grand occasion. I relished spending these special times with my father. Even though there was not much talk between us this was acceptable, because this was better than not having him at all. I learned rather young to make allowances and compromises for some people, something I would continue to do with some of my later relationships. To have someone in my life for a few moments or a short time was better than not having someone at all, especially when dating or in a relationship with a man.

~*~

My father died suddenly was the time I was just starting to get to know him a bit better. My mother was protective of him and she explained to us children that we needed to leave him alone when he came home from work. She also demanded we were not to sit in his living room chair; that was for him, when he arrived home tired from a full day's work. She said, "Kids, your father is coming home. I want you to pick up around the house and do not sit in his chair. Leave him alone when he gets home." I am sure she was aware of his fragility and maybe even his depression. When my father came home from work, and we were all sitting around the dinner table for our evening meal, my mother usually would ask my father, "How was work today?" He would always answer, without exception, "Lousy."

~*~

My father died in March, just one week before my twentieth birthday. From my recollection, everything went so fast. It was like a whirlwind as I remember the whole ordeal. Life certainly has its precious moments and this was not one of them; so much needed to be said. Time made no allowances for this. In preparation for my birthday, he and my mother had already purchased a plaid blue and white skirt with an edge of dark blue piping and blouse ensemble. Even though I wore it infrequently, I kept it for an especially long time, knowing that my father had picked it out for me.

~*~

What I eventually found out later in my research was that my father had a quantity of crippling emotional problems; he was fearful and withdrawn, and experienced clinical depression. He neglected medical attention. I can still see him sitting outside of our house staring out into thin air while smoking a cigarette. He preferred being alone and had few social relationships. His entire life was disrupted and put into an upheaval due to his imprisonment at Dachau and having to flee his country. Both, of course, were major losses. The brutal Nazi persecution and his experiences increased and entrenched his fear and depression.

Memoir of a 2G

# PARENTS

When a person wants to move to another country of his or her own will, that is one scenario. There is yet another situation when one moves to another country for one's own survival, to escape from prejudice, murder and war. My parents came to the United States because of all three; circumstances were stressful in dealing with their fear, and trepidation, and what would be their eventual fate. They hoped that by coming to America they would be free, to live without fear of being murdered, of having all their belongings confiscated and without constant fear of being the next one being exterminated. America empowered my father and mother by giving them freedom.

The German area where my mother emigrated from was either deemed Germany or Poland, and what is now Poland. The eastern provinces of Prussia were a part of the German Empire that Bismarck founded. My mother became Polish overnight due to the different wars and the territory demarcations. When my mother was around German speaking people, I would hear her say, "*Ich bin in Preußen geboren,*" ("I was born in Prussia.")

Neither one of my parents ever went back to their country of origin. They never even mentioned that they wanted to go back. Unlike my parents, my father's sister went back every few years, (something I could not understand, because of what she also went through). I have a better understanding currently why my parents did not want to go back to Germany. Standing on German soil would have brought back too many painful memories. It would have been heart wrenching with too much pain and anger for them to encounter.

My father and mother originated from two completely different parts of Germany, each one of them speaking High German. They each had a slightly different dialect from one another. My mother consistently reprimanded my father w

hen they were communicating, that he was not speaking German correctly. She used to disagree and argue with him on how certain German words ought to be pronounced. He would give in to her so there would be no further bickering.

When my father and mother fought in their relationship, they spoke in German so that we would not understand; it probably was much easier for them to communicate their feelings in their mother tongue. They quarreled later in the evening rather than in the daytime. The differences in my parents' upbringing and backgrounds augmented the tensions between each of them. Not only had my father's experiences traumatized him, but my mother was highly affected by the losses of her family and the Nazi regime.

It makes sense to me now why my parents acted the way they did. Their choices were limited. I have spent most of my life wondering, questioning, and trying to figure things out. Now I get it! In a way I have felt as though I have come full circle. Humanity can play many games and I was caught up in all the moves one makes on a game board, finally landing and winning a space on Peace. With all the time I have used trying to figure things out, I have come to terms with what happened.

~*~

How and where my father and mother met one another could take on many scenarios in my imagination. Neither one of my parents ever talked about their wedding day, ever, nor have I ever seen any wedding pictures of them. They ultimately met on the Upper West Side of Manhattan after they arrived in the United States; my father arrived in the United States in 1937, and my mother in 1938. They got married by a justice of the peace at the town hall in downtown Manhattan on April 26, 1940. I was able to locate their marriage certificate which was interesting to obtain, especially when I had absolutely no idea where or when they got married. On the form they filled out, my mother and father indicated neither was married before. Thank goodness for the records kept by the City Clerk's Office in Manhattan! This was the document that verified that they had resided on the Upper West Side near one another. Neither parent ever told me.

Never in my wildest dreams would I have thought that I would find out this thrilling information about my mother and father. I was so excited to finally know where my parents met and when they married.

As to how they actually met one another I am still curious. I like to imagine that possibly my father sauntered up to my mother and started a conversation and then asked her out or that he said, "Hello," and it went from there. Or maybe they met while walking beside the Hudson River, sitting on benches at Riverside Park, or just plain walking on the street. Or did someone introduce them to one another? I have wondered about what activities my father and mother indulged in, how they got acquainted to better themselves and how they got to understand the American way of life. (For my mother's story about this, see, Page 179).

~*~

After my parents got married they moved to Upstate New York in a rather tiny area in the country, far away from any small town or large city. How they ever found this location, I have no idea. They were foreigners, and who helped them make this journey is a mystery to me. I retrieved a piece of information from a letter that my mother once wrote stating she was aware of being observed by government officials because of her German accent. The public was alerted to the likelihood that some American citizens might be informants with the possibility they might be siding with communists and working against the United States government.

My mother's neighbors were suspicious of her because there were no other people around that vicinity who had a German accent other than her and my father. They were concerned that she might be an informant for the communists. This was the time of the McCarthy Era, in the early nineteen fifties, where suspicion ran high in the questioning of people's loyalty to the United States after the war. This was especially true for people who may have sounded differently than those who were originally born in the States.

My father and mother wanted to have tranquility in their lives, to be surrounded by nature, reside within a safe environment with no one around them, and have a chance to start a new life. This is strictly speculation on my part. My parents' style of living in secluded areas is evident from the different residences we lived in while I was growing up. In my late teens though, our whole family moved again, but this time finally to a city, Albany, New York. This new type of urban atmosphere was definitely unfamiliar, and it took some getting used to. Gone were the wild flowers, green moist grass, sparkling bright stars, peace, quiet, and the respite that all the abundant nature had provided me while residing in the bucolic location I had been accustomed to.

~*~

Assimilating to this country's culture came differently for each one of my parents, especially my father, who had much difficulty acclimating and dealing with the American way of life. He continually spoke about how great Germany was, even with what he went through. He said that living in Munich was so much better than living in America. Even though he was incarcerated for twenty-two months in Dachau, there was this love and loyalty towards his past Germanic way of living, and his love of the German culture. This was true in spite of where he came from was prejudiced against Jews. His adoration for Munich I had difficulty understanding. It is well known that Hitler adored composer Richard Wagner. My father loved opera, and it annoyed my mother to no end that he loved Wagner, especially after what he endured in his life during that regime. You could hear opera blaring at my home on Sunday afternoons on WQXR. I thought that everybody listened to this!

~*~

How my parents had the financial means to survive in Manhattan when they arrived in the late nineteen thirties baffles me. I try to imagine either one of them converting Reischsmark, (the form of currency in 1937), into United States currency, the difficulty they may have encountered.

Did either one of them have any wealth before their arrival into the United States, or did some wonderful people financially help them on their way? From some information I have found, I believe Dad may have come from a middle class family, though much, if not all assets and his residence were confiscated. I found out that his eight-room home in Munich comprised two living rooms, four bedrooms, one kitchen and one storage room. He never got anything back nor did he receive restitution from the German government; his home and his assets were never returned! I understand why my father was the way he was- very quiet, reserved, depressed and often times not present.

~*~

My mother's relationship with my father seemed awkward, they did not communicate well. They argued or said nothing at all. My father did not have deep conversations with her for years. I felt they might not have been close, because I never heard them say loving things to one another and I never saw them kiss or hug, ever. Whether my mother loved my father and vice versa, I have often wondered. There were rather few apparent physical displays of affection towards one another. In one way they were together, yet in another they seemed distant from one another. My father either did not want to communicate or was unable to. This is only my perception. For sure there was this unspoken type of respect towards one another. Just before he died, there was a shift in my parent's relationship; my father was beginning to speak and communicate with my mother. She felt there was hope, because he started to acknowledge her. Then he died. Despite their arguing or bitterness, they had four children.

~*~

As a family we never went on vacations. I would hear kids in school talk about going on vacation around the holiday seasons. I was not aware that this was a common experience for many families and soon realized they took a week or two off to go camping, visit relatives in other states, or go to the Walt Disney amusement park. My family outings consisted of jumping into our car and driving to a swimming area within an hour of our home.

On Sundays our whole family would pile into our Chevrolet and go for long rides in the country to go antiquing. My father and mother would pick up second hand furniture. My mother had an excellent eye; this would present the golden opportunity of bringing a new addition to our home. She would fix, sand, refinish, and lacquer what was purchased; we would then acquire some good-looking furniture. My father always did the driving, since my mother did not drive. Not until years after my father died, did my mother learn how to drive. I have to give him credit for all his patience, because we had to depend on him taking us everywhere. We never stopped to eat at a restaurant, not even to get ice cream, no matter how hot it was. This was before air-conditioning units were installed in automobiles. I enjoyed going on these antiquing excursions, because it was something extraordinary. I usually spent my days roaming around in the fields, woods or I stayed home. To this day I go to flea markets, antique shops, and garage sales. Although there is nothing I want or need at this point of my life, I once in a while pick up something that I know has some value, a special treasure.

~*~

In my former years, my father and mother subscribed to and read the German Jewish Journal *Aufbau*. They would be able to read maybe news of their hometowns in Europe, and catch up on much of the news of what happened to family and friends. This was the one connection they had to their past.

~*~

My mother, not knowing how to drive, depended solely on my father to take her every-where, to help her buy groceries, and to help with errands that occurred in everyday life. We all depended upon him, the only one with a driver's license to take us around to our respective appointments. Grocery shopping was a big ordeal; about every three weeks we took a trip to the market. It would take lots of time because of the distance from our house; time to purchase provisions of meat, chicken, vegetables and cleaning supplies. Expressways were not built yet in our region, so traveling took forever it seemed; we resided in a vicinity where there were two lane roads and back roads. Once home, we emptied the car of all the brown shopping bags filled with groceries and these bags were placed all over the kitchen floor. My job was to reach into each bag and hand my mother the various food so that she could put them in their proper place in the cupboard, refrigerator and large freezer.

~*~

"Ladies and gentlemen: The story you are about to hear is true. Only the names have been changed to protect the innocent." This program, an American television series called Dragnet, was about a Los Angeles police detective named Sergeant Joe Friday who arrested all sorts of suspects and criminals. Hearing that statement on the television screen in the early and late nineteen-fifties on a Thursday evening was thrilling to see and hear. It was unusual for us to watch television, especially a program such as this. Our whole family would visit another family that lived close by. This family also came from Europe. I believe my father and mother felt at home visiting them. This was probably because of the familiarity of being with those people who would understand them and vice versa.

My mother censored everything that we were to read, see or experience. I looked forward to visiting this family because we were allowed to look at TV by ourselves, without parents in tow. The parents would sit in the other room carrying on in deep conversation and I mean deep. This was one time that I felt I had the freedom to sit in front of a TV and take it all in. If my mother had the slightest inkling what we were watching, she would have gone through the roof. They must have been talking about some truly serious stuff in order that she did not interfere or inspect what we were viewing. Not to be under my mother's scrutiny was unusual. She usually kept tabs on us all, making sure we were obedient and toeing the line. This was one time I felt free and fascinated, watching TV. It was thrilling to watch all this drama; of killing, danger, police, and robbery and to hear the exciting music in the background. The show was electrifying and this was a totally new and exciting experience.

~*~

My parents befriended a couple whose names were Henry and Poldi, to whom our family got close to while we resided in the country. They too were refugees, and I also sense that my father and mother felt a special kinship with them because of their history. They spoke in German. They emigrated from Vienna and landed in America just as my parents did. My parents talked a great deal with them, probably feeling relatively comfortable that they too came from Europe. Poldi was a quiet, humble and thin woman whereas her husband Henry was frisky, thin and quick-witted. The Viennese cooking they shared with us was exceptional. The chocolate torte cakes Poldi baked were delicious and memorable. After Henry died, Poldi moved to Albany.

~*~

Easter time, while living in the country, my family used to have Easter baskets filled with all kinds of fantastic goodies such as chocolate bunnies wrapped in pretty colored light blue, pink and yellow tin foil, jelly beans of every imaginable color and sweet chocolate covered marshmallow eggs. My father and mother would hide these baskets behind a tree or bush near our home for each one of us children to find. Games of hide and seek looking for the beautifully adorned Easter baskets was fun and exciting, something that was unusual for us children to participate in. I seldom had so many goodies all at once; I was not brought up with much candy. I find it interesting that my parents did this because this was not a Jewish custom at all. This may have been a way of showing us kids just how much they loved us.

~*~

On special holidays, friends would come over to our home when it was time for a Passover Seder, Thanksgiving or Chanukah. My mother would prepare roast lamb, roast beef, or tongue that would be served as a main dish along with potatoes, sweet potatoes, beans, and more. This would be one of the few times when there was so much food to be had at our table. It was a blast and there was much happiness at these festivities. To be surrounded by these people other than my immediate family was a lively occasion; there was so much joy eating and talking.

# GRANDPARENTS

For numerous years I have often wondered about my grandparents. They were deceased, and I never met them. In my possession I have letters that came from my German paternal grandparents that were sent to him and his sister. My father and his sister had already been living in the United States. The letters were meticulously hand written in German with exceptionally beautiful cursive handwriting on thin off-white tissue paper inserted in thin, gray toned envelopes. The recognizable black swastika logo was stamped on the letters in deep block print. My aunt passed them on to me for safekeeping, and I packed them away, never giving them any more thought.

Communication between my paternal grandparents and my father and aunt (his sister), across the many miles continued from Germany to New York, and then eventually it stopped. My aunt no longer received further correspondence from either one of my grandparents. They were murdered, exterminated in Riga Concentration Camp.

Eventually I had these letters translated into English. They were written lightheartedly as though it was just another ordinary, safe, beautiful day for them, that nothing was wrong. My grandparents did not indicate their unhappiness or the death that would eventually befall them. I believe they were aware the Nazis were intercepting correspondence heading for the United States and elsewhere, so they did not write something that would signal anything unusual or telling that might jeopardize their lives. Their demise finally did arrive. To have lived under such strict and precarious conditions certainly had its toll on the human existence.

These letters that reached the United States were stamped in German and bold black letters spelling the word *"Geoffnet."* This means, "Opened." The stamp indicates that these letters were indeed intercepted, opened, read, and censored by the Nazis, before they were sent across the seas to the United States. The Nazis were always looking for information that they could muster to use against people and have a reason to put them in a concentration camp. Nazis and authoritative participants would be looking for any information that might be written against the Nazi regime, and the German government. Certainly the Nazis also put people in concentration camps for no reason at all or for the slightest infraction. They had the power to allow someone to live or die. That is inarguable, and the obvious outcome was death.

The scope of annihilation of a people is so beyond my comprehension. To hate in such a volume is beyond my understanding. The thought and realization of what happened to my parents and other people during the Holocaust hurts that human beings can have such a hateful capacity to want to get rid of a whole race of people! The devastation for everyone involved was monumental, not only for Jews.

# MY STORY

Memoir of a 2G

## My Youth

Advantages as well as disadvantages are given to any life situation. In the country I was able to roam freely, discover nature, and would eat homegrown vegetables and fruit from our garden. Country fields had beautiful trees that were in bloom. There were dank smells after a rain and there were wild animals that were free to roam. The disadvantage of living in the country is that on a social level I learned much later than my peers on how to communicate. I did not have any friends; I was brought up in the country where it was isolated. Unlike many kids while they grew up, I did not have outside influences from neighbors or peer groups on learning how to act and converse with children my age. Speaking of being a late bloomer, I did not learn how to tell time and ride a two-wheel bicycle until I was thirteen years old. Not surprisingly, in each situation I found it awfully difficult to accomplish, especially learning how to tell time. The younger one is, the more easily a child can pick up such things. But, eventually I did. It was a challenge, to be sure.

Wandering around in the woods gave me the freedom and liberty to do what I wanted. It was great being surrounded with natural and beautiful settings, and all the aromas and sites of plants, flowers, meadows, birds and wild animals. Sunnyboy, our cocker spaniel, having light caramel colored matted clumps of fur, was a great companion and always followed my siblings and me wherever we walked. He would bathe and roll around in the smelly skunk cabbage in the warm dank swamp and then come out and shake his nimble body. We would get slightly wet from the water flying about. He was a joy to have with me, and I think he too loved being around us children. Playing, observing and just plain walking around in the woods got me close to nature's beauty. I would observe plants such as the jack-in-the-pulpit that begin to sprout up with its beautiful dark purple and beige petals in summer days. I would also notice the captivating smell of wild red sweet strawberries. They sprouted up from the deep field of luscious, green grass.

~*~

Growing up as a youth and residing in the country in upstate New York was a beautiful experience. My siblings and I roamed the untilled land in the idyllic countryside and picked wild berries as sweet as sugar. We also found and picked wild strawberries in the deep moist meadow grasses. These strawberries left telltale signs on my fingers with a pinkish tint stain. Luscious currants were picked from the low bushes. We picked wild flowers with sweet smelling aromas and observed all the various wild animals that roamed freely in the fields and forest. Often times I would just lie down in the meadow with my back to the warm stony and grassy ground and gaze above at the gorgeous space with its bluish hues called the heavenly sky. It was a peaceful presence, that was for sure, although at the time I had no idea how peaceful it was. I thought everyone experienced this kind of tranquility. Our closest neighbor was a quarter of a mile away from our home, and we lived a mile and a half off the two lane major highway.

A big part of my life to this day involves surrounding myself with nature. It still supplies me with serenity and a vast appreciation for all its beauty. My enjoyment of flora and fauna, and learning the numerous names of wild flowers, plants, trees and the different animals that I come into contact with is fun. In the past, I enjoyed watching the small murky dank smelling pond next to my home, where polliwogs become frogs. Inspecting all the different stages of larva on its way to becoming a frog was certainly an exciting event to see; every few days I went to the pond to watch this magnificent occurrence.

Picking wild flowers such as daisies, Black-eyed Susans, Queen Anne's lace and violets, placing them in a canning jar filled with water was something I did in the springtime and throughout the summers. Even though many of the wild flowers were tiny, their aromas were powerful, pungent, and sweet. The Adirondack Mountains with their luscious gold, red-orange, red and yellow trees poked out in the autumn, radiating spectacular beauty always.

~*~

My involvement and interest in Girl Scouts led me to receive the Curved Bar, the highest achievement that one can attain in scouting. I attended Girl Scout Camp for two weeks each summer in the Southern Adirondacks. Attending camp was fun in some ways and in others it was not. I was quiet, shy, and socially awkward; I did not meld in with the popular girls or the in-group in camp. My social skills were fairly limited, and I felt ill at ease especially early on in my years while attending this camp. This was new territory for me. The arts and crafts period I liked: I was good at weaving, making linoleum block prints and making a sixteen-strand lanyard. When it came to mail call, I was always looking forward to receiving correspondence from either one of my parents or maybe even my siblings but that seldom happened. Many of my peers received letters often. Only occasionally would I get a postcard from my parents.

One summer when I arrived home from Girl Scout Camp, I had a wonderful time lounging outside in my backyard on the soft, beautiful, warm, verdant green lawn. I was devouring one half of a watermelon my parents gave me as a welcome home present. Its color was lipstick pink, and its sweetness was scrumptious. This was unusual because food was usually doled out in minimum quantities and here I was with one half of a huge wonderful fruit, and it was only for me!

~*~

Frequently I walked barefoot outside on the soft verdant green grass and on one occasion I stepped on a garter snake. Another time I stepped on a bee and got stung and yet on another I walked in a shallow, muddy, slushy swamp. My mother usually insisted that all of us kids had to stay outside and play and not come in or out of the house. Once out, we were to stay out. She was rather insistent on that.

~*~

Veering off of the road next to our home was a dirt road. When it rained the road washed out, creating potholes, while in winter there were many inches of snow piled up in heaps from each heavy downfall. My mother would call the town to have them plow so that a car could travel on the road; the workers would eventually get at it and plow away the snow. It took some time for a snowplow to come through to get rid of the accumulated snow.

~*~

Growing up in the country, I had no other children with whom to play and mingle with other than my two brothers and sister. Rural living was certainly much different than that of a city. I did not have opportunities to join clubs, organizations, with the one exception of the Girl Scouts. While I was in the outdoors or alone in my room, I learned to amuse myself. Playing with my dolls, dollhouse and creating art were my usual pastimes.

~*~

I have the desire to seek out flowers still now. While walking on the streets of Manhattan, I am able to see beauty behind a trellis made out of metal wrought iron fencing and in city parks. I have been able to photograph some gorgeous sites. Even though there are department stores and shops with exceptional merchandise, nothing can compare to the background of capturing stunning areas such as Central Park and the small parks in Manhattan with all their beautiful flowers. Between two pieces of concrete I have seen some minute flowers pop up. Even if some of these are weeds, I still find them beautiful; not only because of their color, but also because of their shape. This gives credence to something greater than me. Nature balances her products out so beautifully.

## My Mother and I

My mother's control included how I dressed, what I said, and how I acted. And there was no room for deviation. I was her dutiful, oldest daughter and learned early on to toe the line. She brought me up to call her Mother, not Mom or Ma, and she was firm about that. What she told me to do I did, so she would not scold me. She instilled much fear in me when she got furious. I do not remember if she hit me, but I did not want her to lay a hand on me. In this type of environment, there was little room for frivolity and fun; seriousness and hard work always had to be accomplished. Her attitude aided her everlasting strength and resilience. I searched for a sign of endorsement from her. Just once I yearned for her approval. Just once! Today I find it is easy for me to want to accomplish things to perfection, and I can slip into that mode in a New York minute!

I would imagine what had happened to my mother and father and to the rest of my family that perished. As far as I could find out, there were ten family members that succumbed to the devastation of the Nazis and perished in concentration camps. I am saddened that I did not get to know my mother and that she did not get to know me. I was curious about my background and confused not knowing much of anything. The past just was not talked about at all. What a void!

~*~

Even after I was out of high school and living at home, my mother did not allow me to dress in the type of clothing that divulged my body shape in any way. I purchased two brand new mustard and army green chino straight skirts that were folded and put in a bag on the back porch waiting to get ironed. I never saw them again to wear even once! She probably threw them out or gave them to someone. There may have been two reasons for this. One, my mother did not like the mustard, yellowish army green color because it reminded her of the Nazis. And two, no daughter of hers was going to run around in a straight skirt that just might reveal her body shape, that was for sure. Makeup, lipstick and nail polish of any colors were unheard of.

~*~

On this one occasion, I was sitting out in the backyard of our home sunning myself; my mother walked down the steps of the back porch of my house and actually sat down beside me. This happened seldom. Actually it sort of freaked me out, it was so unusual. I thought she was going to reprimand me about something. She started talking to me about my sister, who at the time was starting to wear eye makeup. She said, "Your sister looks like a hussy." These were her exact words! I never knew my mother to use such a word, "hussy," and that word sounded pretty horrendous to me. I proceeded to explain to her that my sister was ok wearing eye makeup and that she will outgrow doing that. She was just being an experimental teenager and doing what other kids in her peer group did and stating that it was harmless. I was shocked to hear my mother's judgmental opinion and attitude about my sister and hoped that what I said would soften the weight of her thought process. I was intrigued that my mother spoke to me in this way. It was rather unusual for her to reach out to me in the manner that she did. I liked it and I almost felt like a peer of hers, or that she thought that I was mature enough in that she could talk to me in this manner. It was a highly unusual experience. My sister was five and a half years younger than I. Being the first born, I was not allowed to do or get away with things that my sister got away with. My mother was much stricter with me.

~*~

My mother taught and instilled in me to have class and act like a "lady." I was supposed to have impeccable manners. To do otherwise, well, there were absolutely no other options. Any other way was "*verboten,*" and there certainly would be repercussions. No matter what environment I was in, she would tell me loud and clear that I was talking inappropriately, no matter who was around.

She made sure that I was always poised, sitting correctly, and that I had good posture. One of her mantras was, "Pick up your feet when you walk." Another was, "Sit up straight and don't slouch when you eat." And yet another was, "Don't talk with your mouthful, don't slurp." It was important to her that my manners and physicality were impeccable and god forbid if I strayed! Experimentation of any kind was out of the question for me!

~*~

I would notice the way girls would have their hair cut and styled. I wanted the type of hairstyles they had. Not only was their hair coiffed beautifully, but they also had interesting haircuts. Or let me just say that these girls' hair looked much differently than the way I had my hair styled. When my hair needed trimming or cutting, my hairstylist was none other than my mother. She would cut my hair in a way that I felt was unattractive and different from the other girls around me. I felt embarrassed about the way I looked. I looked different from my peers in that most of them were blue eyed, had blond hair and fair complexions. She gave me pigtails when I was young, and when I was older in junior high and high school, my hair was cut the way she wanted it cut. She would hack my hair or so I thought, and create bangs on my forehead in a simple pageboy that made me look like a young girl. I did not like it, but what could I do?! I never thought to go contrary to anything she said. I obeyed her implicitly. I was aware of the consequences, such as her strictness, yelling, and the fear that I had of her hitting me. That was the way it was. To be unable once in a while to experience and experiment with my own creativity on how I felt about things left an indelible mark that I am well aware of.

~*~

My mother made most of my clothing. I did not have any options of what I could wear while I went to school. She was opposed to any fashion fads of the time. She forced me to wear what she made and that was that. What I received was hand-me- downs. I wanted to wear what was stylish but that was not an option, and I would feel awkward at times because of my mother's taste in clothing. Even when I attended junior and senior high, lipstick and straight skirts were out of the question. I was never allowed to wear any makeup even for dress up; looking attractive was not an important element that I needed to learn and was not part of my mother's way of bringing me up. I was taught to dress modestly and have modest behavior.

What I hoped for was to be able to dress in the way and style I wanted, to be able to illustrate my creative side by the way I dressed. I did that finally when I had enough money saved up and was on my own. Eventually I sewed my own clothing, knitted attractive sweaters, and haunted thrift stores, giving me many options for a better and original wardrobe.

~*~

It became confusing at times because I was brought up in European and American ways. Trying to acclimate to the American way of life, so different from my parents' way of thinking and doing, conflicted with what many of my peer group were doing. The way I was dressed, the manners I was expected to have, the kinds food I was brought up with, and dating seemed dissimilar to those around me. How my mother and father were bringing me up was from their European worldview and yet they were (I believe) trying to assimilate the best way they knew, attempting to bestow this new worldview of theirs on me as well. What I would hear and see outside of my home was different. For example, so many of my peers were dating or going to the movies or just doing what they wanted to do when they wanted to. Not me! My responsibilities were to be at home, do the housework, take care of my siblings, and clean.

~*~

When I was a child and sometimes dressed in a European style white sock, pigtails and brown laced up shoes, I felt weird, different, and ugly. And why would I have been dressed any other way? My mother would say, "Shoes are made for comfort and support not style," and "Therefore, your feet will not get deformed... School is not a place for dressing up and looking fashionable." No daughter of hers was going to have deformed feet that was for sure! But, does a child or teen ever think like that? Absolutely not! As any teenager will tell you, "I want to fit in and look like the other girls in my class." On occasions when it snowed or rained, I had to wear black galoshes with metal clips, the type men and boys wore, and I stowed them in a barn where we waited for school bus number 6, so that I would not be made fun of by the other kids on the bus. These galoshes made me feel so strange; I was so aware that the girls in my class never wore them. I wanted to fit in, be like them and wear what they wore.

~*~

Mother often said, "Go up and clean your room," or "Go up to your room and read," something that in either case I did not enjoy doing. Having been given a subscription to *Jack and Jill* magazine, I would often only look at the pictures, because to read was such a chore. I did not understand the concept of how to read and retain what I read, nor wanted to, for that matter. I would much rather have made some kind of artwork, play with my dolls, or go running around in the woods. That definitely was so much more fun, rather than sitting and reading words!

Having been brought up with nursery rhymes, the likes of *Humpty Dumpty*, *Jack and Jill* and *Three Blind Mice*, and such stories as *The Three Bears* and *Cinderella*, I often times dreamed about them, but the story of *Cinderella* especially caught my eye and soul, and I questioned how she could ever have been treated that way.

Today, I love the fact that I can actually sit for innumerable hours and get lost in the written word and get so engrossed in a book, finally! I have the fortitude, patience and the total understanding on how to sit and read, hooray! I love it.

~*~

Sometimes my father would have a silly streak in him out of the blue and this was hilarious. Sometimes it was scary to see. It was a rare occasion to see him act like this, to let his personality brighten up. He once licked his plate in front of us children and my mother went bonkers. She was such a strict and serious German woman. And when all of a sudden he would say or do something silly or funny, she would get quite annoyed. How sad! She would say in German, *"Saga das nicht vor den kindern!"* "Do not say that in front of the children!"

To observe this side of my father's personality, I of course loved it, to see him be silly and smile, but it was a rare event indeed.

I was not allowed to be silly. My mother would say, "Don't be silly or I will give you something to be silly about." Presently I realize how difficult it was, because I believe it is natural and in every child's interest to want to have fun and be silly. The seriousness of the atmosphere in our home bred an uneasiness that is difficult to explain.

When I was around five years old, my father drove a Ford Deluxe Series rumble seat coupe manufactured in the late nineteen-thirties. When as a family we were traveling somewhere, he turned the engine off as the car went descending down from the top of the hill, and just let the car coast down. Though my mother was a bit scared as well as I, he knew what he was doing. He was fooling around and just smirked. I think he wanted to irk my mother.

My upbringing was stern and firm; to be responsible, do things correctly and immediately. I had better not make any mistakes or else! This mindset I learned so well so young. I was often afraid to make a mistake. It stopped me from trying new and different things while growing up. This followed me into adulthood once I was on my own and later on in life. I had the courage to try new things much later in life. I was able to break the old mindset and became more daring to do things without all that fear. Examples of some of risks I took were: opening up my own company, moving to the Southwest all by myself, and not knowing anyone, and finally, finishing up my Bachelor's Degree in my "late" young age, all of which came out well.

~*~

Once I angered my mother because of my sister. While the latter was attending junior high school, I had already graduated from high school and was working a full-time job. My sister got the bright idea of purchasing a motor scooter and came to me asking if I would be willing to cosign a sales agreement, thinking I would have some extra money to spare to help her out financially. Under the notion that she had already run it by our mother for approval, I had no problem signing it and said, "Sure I would be happy to do that for you." The contract was signed, sealed and delivered! My sister was the proud owner of a beautiful blue Vespa that was in perfect condition. The story does not end there. Not long after this purchase, she ran it into the side of a teacher's car parked on a city street. I never heard the end of it. Our mother was furious! So now I was the guilty one; `without this loan that I cosigned for my sister this mishap would never have occurred. And all throughout this episode, I thought that my mother had approved of this purchase! That ends the vehicle story, not with a happy ending, but thank goodness no one got seriously hurt.

~*~

Topics such as boys, sex or relationships weren't ever talked about or explained to me. My mother would come up with some strange strong statements and messages such as, dating or going out with boys was for after I graduated from high school. I wondered if this was her experience coming from her background or was this just the way she was going to bring me up. Neither one of my parents was strict about whom I would date later on, in other words, the guys that I dated did not have to be Jewish. One of my girlfriend's parents did not like that idea and did not want their daughter to hang around with me for fear their daughter would date a Gentile man. The thing they had not yet known was that their daughter was already dating non-Jewish guys! And without my help, either! I am grateful that my mother did not bring me up prejudiced. While growing up, we had friends from all walks of life, different religions and backgrounds who visited my home. I had to learn through trial and error, my own experiences, and the various paths I took, what constituted a happy and workable relationship.

~*~

I became aware that my friends and acquaintances had the immense fortune of having parents who played with them when they were young, as well as having a communicative relationship. My experience was so much different than theirs in that neither one of my parents had the time, inclination, or understanding to play with me. The only exception is when on occasion, my whole family would get together to play Monopoly, but this usually only happened when there was a couple that came over for dinner. Afterwards we all would be happy and play board games.

I had to fend for myself, without any help from my parents. I am not complaining, just stating a fact. I did not know that it was customary for parents to help and be there for their offspring. When I observe parents with their college age sons and daughters going out together, planning for college, all those experiences seem very foreign to me.

~*~

When my mother passed away December 31, 1996, I felt a sense of tranquility and a certain type of relief. It felt as though a burden had been lifted and there was calm surrounding me. I felt there would be some liberation and no more criticism. I feel awkward, revealing this now, but it is the truth. All this disapproval and negativity were finally going to come to a standstill, and I certainly welcomed that form of peace, something that I have wanted for a long time. Unlike when my father died, this was a different sort of feeling of loss and somewhat welcoming. When my father died, I missed him so much. Today I miss my mother too for all that she taught and gave me spiritually and educationally. This included types of living skills, such as how to take care of a home, a garden, not giving up on anything, and to do what you do with pure perfection. Today I have the ability and proficiency to know how to communicate with her and not get so riled up by what she would say. I would have taken more risks to speak to her and get answers. Is that called maturity?! I would have liked her to see what I have become and what I have achieved.

Memoir of a 2G

## My Father and I

To point out the nature of integrity that my father wanted to instill in me and insist that I have when I was rather young, the following incident I recall rather vividly. He and I went to the department store in town one Sunday morning to get the newspaper. We lived in the country and I was around six years old at the time. This was an unusual event for me as he usually drove to the store alone. Upon entering the store, I noticed at the front register beautifully bright and shiny colored packages of gum that looked so enticing. It was unusual for me to be so enticed because neither did I chew gum nor seldom did I go shopping in any store. So I took one package of gum from the candy display, kept it and put it in my pocket. Dad paid for the newspaper, and we continued home.

I did not receive an allowance, and I was not brought up with chewing gum. Once home my father noticed I had something new in my possession and to my surprise he asked me, "Where did you get the chewing gum?" I said, "I took it off the gum rack at the store." He said, "You can't just take things and not pay for them." He immediately hauled me back into our Chevy, and we went right back to the department store with the contraband. He made me apologize to the storeowner and tell her that I took it without paying and without anyone's permission. The storeowner was kind, whereas my father was furious. This one small example certainly left me with an indelible impression that I can remember clearly to this day. He wanted me to live with a moral compass.

~*~

My father said to me two important things I have remembered distinctly to this day: "Always sit like a lady by keeping both your legs together, and "Carry a dime at all times for an emergency," These were the times without cell phones. There were telephone booths then, located at various street corners. One could walk to a corner, open a glass or plastic door, and in the privacy of this tiny space, place a telephone call for only a dime. My father was a classy man, and I believe his saying this was one of the ways he was able to show me his love the best way he knew how, because as I have described, he said so little to me. The few times he did talk to me left such an indelible impression. His way of teaching was with the least amount of words and getting to the point and without yelling and nagging; there was this simplicity to it all.

The loss of not getting to know my father because of his continued silence left me with a void; I was just getting to know him when I was twenty years old. It is as though he was ripped from my heart. This was my first authentic experience of death of someone close to me; it shocked me. I felt confused on how I was to act. Was I to weep, take care of my mother and siblings? Confusion was wrapped around me like a shroud. Who can ever plan for death! My only reference point of death was the Holocaust. But this was my one and only father. And I had only spoken to him four hours prior to his death over the telephone, and it only made it all the more surreal for me. I had never met my extended family before they perished. But my father, with whom I would sit and paint with at various special times, was gone. I would no longer have the chance, while the warm sun beamed down on us in the lush green meadow, to observe him create beautiful scenery from his empty canvas. No longer would there be smells of turpentine and oil paints. But the memory of him lingers on.

~*~

At a restaurant I was waiting patiently to meet a man, a collector of fountain pens, so that he could look at an old and incredibly handsome fountain pen that I have owned for a long time. With the possibility of having him fix it, I likewise wanted him to give me some information about its origin. It was supposed to have been my father's pen that my mother passed down to me. Roughly forty years I have had it in my possession. Having been a collector of vintage women's handbags, costume jewelry and ladies' compacts, I have not wanted to sell it because of its sleek shiny exquisite brown and black beauty.

The day came to find out if this pen could be restored to its original condition and to obtain any pertinent data on its history. Using a fountain pen was a wonderful way to write letters and cards, something that I have enjoyed doing. This man looked at it and said to me while we were sitting at a small square table in this restaurant filled with many patrons and noise of conversation all around, "Your father's name is on it." Was I astounded! And I almost fell over with joy and never had any idea! With my loupe that I took out of my handbag, I viewed it, and yes, right on the side of this pen stamped horizontally was his name with the year "37." July 16, 1937 was the date that he arrived in this country. As the man was explaining all this to me, I suddenly started to tear up realizing that never until now had I known this. This man was able to find out the name, type and other important identifying information regarding this pen's history.

Since this meeting I have often wondered who may have bought this pen for my father. I will never get an answer to this conundrum. What I do know is that one week from now I will have in my possession this refurbished pen. I had absolutely no idea that his name was engraved on it. I am so thankful that I never got rid of it. What a gift!

# Faith

A Jewish custom is to name a newborn child after a deceased relative in memory of that person. My middle name, Carolyn, was given to me after one such relative, but my first name is not a biblical one whatsoever. It means "a noble one." Throughout my passage in life, I have often been asked how I got this name and whom was I named after. My parents probably wanted me to assimilate and fit into the American culture by giving me an American sounding name. Also, my upbringing was that I was an American first and foremost; that was evident and important to them.

~*~

As a teenager, I had the chance to attend a camp focusing on Reform Judaism and the arts, including music and dance. My mother bought me brand new, lovely clothing for this experience, and pink was my favorite color choice. This was unusual in that my mother would usually make my clothing or I would receive hand me downs. But once in a great while they did purchase something new for me to wear. Having been picked to attend this camp for my art creativity was a positive and enjoyable experience.

The camp was located in the gorgeous Berkshire Mountains in Massachusetts, known for their vast green forests. This was the first time I had the occasion of socializing only with Jewish girls and boys. We wrote and produced a play, learned Jewish and Hebrew songs and dances, and created delightful art. Meeting kids from all over was a pleasant experience. They were so nice, fun to be with, and I adapted well to this new adventure. The fun I had was so incredible that I actually was not looking forward to going home when camp ended. Being at camp essentially gave me another perspective on life that was pleasant and fun. The setting enabled me to employ my talent and I felt I was in a warm and kind atmosphere. The experience of meeting kids from all over the country gave me a way to view how easily I could make friends. Along with this, it also showed me my peer group could accept me.

~*~

When I was an adult, a group trip was planned for three days in Washington, DC to visit the United States Holocaust Memorial Museum and Smithsonian Museum. A rabbi from upstate New York put together this journey that included people from different religions, such as Muslim, Catholic, Protestant, Jewish. At first I was excited to attend because of the possibility of finding some answers to questions that I had. Our group was the first of its kind to attend this museum.

As we got closer to departure time, I started having second thoughts and was actually scared to go with all these people and face a part of my history that I have never been able to talk about nor view in any graphic detail. In the past I was unable to watch movies or read books about the Holocaust or talk about what happened; it was just too close to my heart, and I carried heaps of sadness and fear. There was no one to whom I could turn. Even though I did not realize it at the time, to finally expose my feelings about what had happened and the many secrets of the past that were buried, would have been somewhat difficult to have to deal with.

After I spoke to the rabbi, I still remember his saying to me to this day, "This journey will be good for your healing." Since I trusted and liked this rabbi, I decided to go and not back out. But it was close; I was so scared to face what I thought I might see and hear and learn.

To this day, I especially still remember the exhibit at the Holocaust Museum of all the tiny children's shoes knowing that they had perished. Details of the other exhibits are also etched in my mind. This plain viewing of such information was horrifying and sad. I do not know whether this trip helped me in my healing, but it gave me some relief in knowing a reality and proof of what actually occurred by seeing and hearing all the obvious examples that were shown in the multitude of exhibits, photographs and films.

When we all returned from the museum, having spent many hours there, we sat together in a hotel room and shared as a group whatever was on our minds. Out of this entire group, I was the only one that was a 2G. Even though I found the whole experience emotional and depressing, and was not actually able to articulate my feelings of sorrow, I was able to observe some truth and reality about what actually went on during this horrific moment in world history.

This trip helped to get the help that I needed. Whether this profound and informative trip improved my understanding of what went on, I cannot remember. The group I traveled with was most understanding and compassionate. I also do feel fortunate to have had this opportunity to get the facts that had eluded me for countless years.

# Goals

In my thirties, while attempting to figure out my life, I still had many unanswered questions. To speak about my woes I sought out a therapist/counselor. I chose him because of his expertise in dealing with children. I thought that he would be the perfect match for me to share my thoughts and queries to finally find out some answers. Since I believed that since his work consisted mainly of working with children, he would not only be a good listener, he would also probably be kind and patient, something that was totally out of my sphere of existence. When I met him, yes, he had all these qualities.

One day when I came to his office he asked me simply and frankly, "How do you feel?" He might as well have asked me to recite the alphabet backwards and in Japanese! As he was especially emphasizing the word "feel," I had absolutely no idea of what he was talking about and his kind of question was totally not part of my vocabulary. I became baffled as to what answer he might be expecting. On another occasion I came back to seek his expertise. I mentioned to him that I now understood a small inkling about this feeling stuff. I came to his office and said, "I am upset the way this guy said these things to me." This was progress on my part and a new concept for me. I was accustomed to not say much. I can still hear my mother's voice in the background saying, "A lady is seen but not heard," or "Act ladylike!" It was unusual to be able to tell someone in a safe environment what was going on with me and to have the opportunity to tell someone how I felt about the situation at hand.

As a result of talking with a counselor about some aspects of my life, I learned what it takes for better communication, what constitutes a loving relationship, how to be assertive, and how to express myself without feeling that I may be judged. I had to relearn that if I did something wrong, the world was not going to catch on fire, and that it did not make me a bad person. I learned that there is a difference between who I am and what I do. As I write, this all sounds good and simple on paper, but the practice to continue to live life on life's terms still has its many challenges. However, it also has created an improved life. A saying I once read, "The truth shall set you free," certainly has its merits. I was able to find my truth and my true self. As a result of what I learned, although it was not easy, I was able to work in sales and also start my own business. If that was not a turnaround in my life, I do not know what is!

On my further quest for truth and understanding and achieving the best life possible, I was introduced to 12-step programs; a way of living that has certainly without question enhanced my life. It is a spiritual path that each individual can tailor to his or her own liking. It was exciting to know that I no longer had to feel alone, had to blame, to be angry and I was able to be free of demons. It is a spiritual lifestyle and has helped me through all kinds of life scenarios.

In my rearing I was not allowed to mention anything about how I felt, what I felt or why I felt the way I did. That was *"verboten,"* territory. Too, I led a very sheltered life as a youth. By explaining to this therapist the best way I knew how, about what was going on with me, I was then able to see and somewhat understand how to deal with life on life's terms. It was an awakening take on this new thought process. This new awareness worked especially well when there were difficult times, and these new tools worked for me to cope with life as I saw it. By sharing my most inner secrets and thoughts without being condemned, ridiculed or told to be quiet, I felt grateful that I had someone with whom I was able to explain what was going on in my life for the first time. The truth did set me free somewhat!

~*~

My goals at that time did not include either college or marriage. There were many reasons for this. My dating experience was nil to this point. Having been a late bloomer, I wanted to experience life as most kids had done in their teens.

Given the kind of relationship my parents had with one another, I was unwilling to risk one for myself. Even though I did not like arguing, bickering, and yelling, I figured there was a good possibility that I would repeat these patterns, because they were all that I knew. Because of my parents modeling these behaviors, I did not know any other way of relating. I did not even have many outside role models to provide other options growing up. In spite of all this, I did cultivate some serious relationships much later on. I felt that I was unable to make a concerted commitment at that time. Since my autonomy meant so much to me, I found myself steering away from long-term obligation.

The harmony in nature was my role model for a healthy relationship. I was so connected with the earth, the woods and its beauty. Even though I cultivated some serious relationships much later on, I felt that I was unable and reluctant to make a concerted commitment to these relationships.

~*~

My main motivation after high school was to just make money and be financially stable. I learned that money is a process by which one can acquire goods. I am not my money and I do not put it on a pedestal. At the same time, I do live a lifestyle that pleases me, but I do not have money rule my way of life. I did not want to have a meager life or one devoid of possessions. I thought that acquiring objects was a way of being accepted by my peers and demonstrating I was financially capable. Of course, I eventually learned that this was not the case. The idea of acquiring things and antiques was eventually a burden, and does not put a person in a special limelight. I am not what I own.

In most cases we were not given money to spend as children and did not receive allowances. Money was scarce in my family and making money due to hard work seemed like the most logical and prudent solution for me. Saving and accumulating for my future were important; I was frugal and learned well at a young age to work hard, do chores correctly the first time and thus I would reap the benefits towards achieving positive outcomes. To make something of myself, be productive and become even further self-sufficient, even though I felt I was somewhat of a failure, was what I wanted. I feel saddened that my parents did not create an opportunity to sit down with me early on to teach me some of the rudiments. While I was in my youth, neither my mother nor father ever sat me down to talk about, just for the sake of discussion, anything at all. They were working hard, too busy, or just plain emotionally unavailable.

I did not finish my secondary education because I was restless, full of anxiety, did not have the capacity to memorize, and was unable to write a decent paper. Yet, I was curious about life, very curious in fact. There were few options open to me that would financially allow me a substantial salary. "I do not know what I want to be when I grow up," I would frequently say to my friends and acquaintances, "I do not want to be poor." As a family we did not have "things," material things like other kids, and I wanted to excel to a level where I would acquire and have "things." Now that I have achieved procuring possessions, now what! And now I have the challenge of getting rid of what I have collected for so long, an extensive collection of dolls, costume jewelry, and handbags. Selling and finding a new home for my collections has been an endeavor. It has taken some time to find someone who wants to spend their money to invest in these items. I was able to fulfill almost all that I have yearned or dreamed of and more. Consistent hard work and sacrifice have em-powered me to exist with a contented life.

Memoir of a 2G

## City Living

Our whole family moved to Albany, New York, when I was a teenager in the midst of ninth grade. I eventually got accustomed to the new distractions and noises familiar and unique to urban living. There were no more beautiful starlit nights, sumptuous quiet summer afternoons or sounds of birds that would come around my home's windowsills. It was like learning to live another whole new way all over again, surrounding myself with people and many new choices of things to select from.

My mother kept a strict watch on me and I had to forever be obedient to what she said. There was absolutely no deviation on when I said I would be home, not even one minute past the hour. Punctuality was an important aspect of her living style and she made it an imperative way for me to function in my daily life. Many various responsibilities were added to my teenage life, washing dishes, cleaning, dusting, babysitting, vacuuming, ironing and the list goes on. One of my mother's mantras was, "Stop pussy footing around and do the dishes." Living in the city I was still a quiet, shy and accountable teenager. Since my father and mother were always working, I now had to do more cleaning around the home, watch my siblings, and of course the obvious obligation of attending school. While other kids were having fun and what seemed like not having too much responsibility, or so I thought, I was usually at home doing what had to be accomplished to help with the family chores.

It was not unusual for one of my girlfriends to walk over to my home on a Saturday late morning and ask me if I could go out with them. The answer was a definite "No," because I had to accomplish all my chores around the house.

~*~

After I moved to Albany I used to visit Poldi, a woman who was a friend of my parents and an acquaintance from my youth. We became friendly and she would reminisce about her experiences when she years ago resided in Vienna. She too was able to share some stories about my parents that she remembered. Soft-spoken, with truthfulness, kindness and patience, she answered my queries. She experienced a brave and intriguing past, having been brought up Catholic, and while living in Vienna she met and dated this Jewish man, who then became her husband, Henry. Her immediate family ostracized her for dating him because he was Jewish and not Catholic, and therefore she also had repercussions from her church. She loved him and did not care what they said or how they felt about her relationship with him; she married and lived with Henry for the rest of her life. It was a beautiful love story. I felt privileged to have learned those parts of her poignant narrative.

Poldi was able to give me some information about my family; anything I might learn about my father or mother would be like finding a diamond in the street. It was beautiful. She would on occasion say to me not to end up staying alone in my later life, because being alone has its hardships and sadness. For years I could not comprehend what she was talking about. All I wanted to do at the time was to be footloose and fancy-free, to be free as a bird. I had a great deal of fun. Now I understand. There would be nothing better than to have a partner with whom to share my life. Funny how one is given some clues sometime during their life, and yet, one is unable to understand or relate to what is being said. Now I know.

~*~

I taught at Arbor Hill Community Center in the inner city of Albany. These great kids had vibrancy, enthusiasm and showed a thirst for knowledge. I am also pleased to have had the opportunity of being a Girl Scout leader for a junior troop, and teaching them arts and crafts. I loved teaching kids, and I was delighted to be able to pass on art creativity as well as information on living skills. At first, a few of the children would struggle. They thought that they could not make or do something. I gave them positive feedback and said, "You can do it." They just needed a bit of coaxing, and they would produce fabulous artwork. Remarkable what a little bit of encouragement can do for a child, let alone for anyone.

~*~

Girl Scouts was a major component in my life as I grew up while living in the country and in the city. In scouting I started out as a Brownie Scout and went all the way in receiving the Curved Bar. Working on my Merit badges and then attending Girl Scout camp was one of the chief ways of how I learned to familiarize myself with other girls my age. This organization taught me about life, integrity, to be honorable, to do what is right, and to respect and learn how to care for our land. Even though I was shy and it was difficult to get to know other girls, I still enjoyed scouting. In the rural area where I lived, there were few opportunities to join other kinds of groups, so this one made a big impression on me. Creating art projects and working towards a goal in achieving these badges gave me a form of structure. I accomplished the correct requirements to earn the badges. It made me feel confident and proficient.

The process of earning Merit badges was enjoyable because it gave me self-worth and a sense of purpose with some challenges. Fulfilling these requirements was difficult, but I felt capable of achieving them. Items that I could use for badges were not easily accessible around my home, and I certainly would not ask my mother for things, so it took some ingenuity on my part to come up with ideas to fulfill and finish them. Asking her for most anything was unheard of. She would lecture or inquire no end as to why I would need something, which gave me the inkling that not asking her for items was the better way to go.

While I lived in the city, I became a Girl Scout leader and met girls from all walks of life, different religions and nationalities. The troop met in an inner city area with girls coming from varied ethnic backgrounds. The opportunity of having a Girl Scout troop of my own was a great feeling in that I was able to present examples to show them how to live the best possible way, to instill art in their lives and just share with them the rudiments for obtaining healthy and good living.

On one occasion I was able to send two girls to an overnight and serene Girl Scout camp for the weekend that was situated in a beautiful wooded area. I chose two girls that I felt needed this experience the most and that under any other circumstance would not have had this wonderful opportunity. They would not have had the financial means to afford it. They would have a spectacular once in a lifetime experience, and they would have the joy of their lives.

~*~

While in my teens, I had the surprise of my life. Upon my arrival home from school, I opened the front door, and all of a sudden all these girls yelled out in unison, "Surprise!" Boy, was I shocked and had absolutely no idea this surprise was going to happen. It had never occurred to me that there would be a party, a sweet sixteen party, let alone for me. What was so sweet about being sixteen anyway? To me it had been just another day. It was unusual being around so many girls my age and from what I remember, after I got over the initial shock and was not embarrassed anymore, we had fun talking and eating cake.

To have all these girls in my home to surprise me without my ever knowing what they were up to and that they had secretly planned this occasion shocked the heck out of me. I always had this feeling that one of my closest girlfriends came up with the idea of my party. I have a friend since ninth grade, and she told me that my mother and another gal were the ones that put this party together.

That my mother was part of this scheme surprised me, because I would never have realized that she thought this was such a special occasion for a daughter to celebrate. For my mother and my friends to have kept a secret from me for so long was definitely incredible. I did not know how to react in this situation; I felt weird, wondering why someone would want to make such a celebration for me. Being the center of attention, I felt awkward and shy. Hiding under a rock would have been preferable. It all went well, and of course, my mother baked the greatest cake ever for all of us to enjoy. I began to understand that this passage for a girl to become a woman was symbolized in the American culture by having her sixteenth birthday, and so the sweet sixteenth celebration.

~*~

Throughout my youth I had been shy, reserved and unobtrusive. I was not the most popular girl nor did I date, which led me to a quiet and reserved existence socially and romantically. In most cases, after the school day ended, I went straight home. On a few occasions I volunteered at the pediatric ward at Albany Medical Center. I also was a Candy Striper and I was quite proud of being one. Candy Stripers did everything a nurse did other than provide injections, needles and medication to the patient.

~*~

My youngest brother and I went swimming in a gorgeous cerulean blue clear lake. We grabbed two metal light green chairs to sit on located next to the beach, and placed all our swimming gear, food, and towels on the warm soft sand. After sitting a while I decided to swim out to the raft in the lake, leaving my brother back on the beach to play in the sand next to the chairs. After a while, I swam back to find our chairs gone! Two guys took them without my brother's consent; they would not listen to him nor did they care what he said. He was quite young, so when they saw this young kid they thought they could do what they pleased. I took care of that incident! Walking over to them, I asked if they took our chairs, they nodded. I said, "I need the chairs that you took from my brother!" They looked at me with disdain and they acted as though they were not going to move. I repeated loudly, "*Give back the two chairs that you took from us!*" I was not going to be intimidated by either one of them; I even thought to whack one of them. Taking advantage of a little kid was beyond my thinking. They finally acquiesced, letting me take them back. My brother and I continued having a wonderful relaxing afternoon swimming. What bullies!

~*~

I am more inclined to be a bit of a serious type of person rather than a silly one. However, when my brother who is two years younger than I have gotten together, I usually have exploded in laughter. I would have tears running down my cheeks. He has this Jerry Lewis form of humor, with ridiculous clowning around, and an outgoing personality at times.

He and I went grocery shopping and you would have thought I was attending a comedy club, except this happened right in the grocery and dry foods aisles. His actions and talking to other customers while we were walking up and down grocery aisles shopping for food put me in hysterics. He has this ability to get other people laughing. His silliness and antics have been contagious. One example was when he went up to someone he did not know and struck up a conversation; my brother got them laughing by making all these funny gestures. Laughter can be such contentment; there is no question.

# School

Challenges and obligations of any teacher are to pass on to a student the understanding of the topic. Provided the student has the ability and reasoning capacity to understand and learn a new subject, there is no reason why a teacher would be unable to teach a student to understand a subject.

In my youth I had an agonizing and challenging time understanding a subject totally foreign to me. I was a slow learner. The concepts were unfamiliar then and even as I write this today, I have the slightest understanding of the subject Math Ten. I twinge to think about it; it just did not add up.

After speaking to a knowledgeable person in the education field, I came to realize that some teachers do not have the ability to make clear on how their subject works. This was completely true with some of my teachers. Until now I thought that I did not have the ability to learn. But no! After speaking with him, I finally realize that I was cheated out of having teachers able to fully explain how a subject works, and make the subject make sense to me. Wow, what a revelation.

Having had the honor of taking Math Ten over three times, I still do not have the grasp or the understanding of it even today. The student suffers, maybe thinking that he or she may lack in some learning capacity when in fact it was the teacher that had the problem of being unable to explain a certain concept. This new information astounded me. The thought did cross my mind that maybe I was stupid; I did not have the ability to understand the subject. What a relief to learn that I could have possibly passed Math Ten, the first time after all, provided I had a teacher better equipped to explain the subject.

How many other children have felt this way? From having the experience with this one subject, I feel that it is important to have teachers truly understand their subject matter and have the ability to relate this information to the student. Wow what a revelation! I'm sure I am not alone in feeling this way.

~*~

There is absolutely no question; I did not have the best grades in high school, had difficulty in learning, retaining information and had completely no idea how to memorize. I just could not do it. No matter how much I tried to study, I could not connect the dots. I worked for two years after high school and thought that then I would be able to learn, but these hurdles and complications went on through college. Nothing changed. I was afraid the teacher would call on me. I was also afraid I would lose focus and daydream. Nothing changed, and I had the same challenges and complications as when I initially started school.

Not until later in my life was I able to learn and learn I did! Very late in my life, I finally received my Bachelor of Arts degree and excelled at achieving it. Finishing up my degree meant so much to me!

~*~

Seldom did I receive any positive input from my mother, father, or teachers while growing up. The one exception, however, was my fourth grade art teacher. She gave me constructive criticism and instilled confidence in me. I vividly remember an incident where she told me that I was good in art and that if I kept at it, I could become decent in this field. I almost felt as though she might not be telling the truth, it was so unusual. That assertion is still clear to me now, as my confidence was nil, and I did not feel that good about myself. Rarely, if ever, did I receive compliments from either my mother or father, let alone other teachers. So, this was huge. This incident left an indelible impression upon me then because she embraced the creative side of what I was generating as a child.

~*~

Different stages in my school and college life were challenging for me. Fairly shy and afraid to be called on in class and terrified that I did not know the answer to the question being asked by the teacher, made me feel awfully scared. If it were left up to me, I would not have attended school at any cost. But, that was not reality, was it? After some time the words would blur together, one sentence after another. It did not click with me. On the bright side though, there were kids to communicate with even though I was usually so reserved.

Teaching takes practical and knowledgeable experience. Another component is being kind. My father was kind but did not have the knowledge of how to teach me to add numbers. While attending first or second grade, I would sit down with him and we would do flash cards in simple arithmetic to hopefully have me learn and understand how to add. I would get these flash cards and he would ask me, "What is 7 + 7?" I would answer him, "14!" But, when it was 7 + 8, I just did not have a clue. He would then ask me, "8 + 8?" I would answer him with joy, "16!" But, when he asked, "8 + 9," I was as perplexed as ever. Unlike the way kids are being taught now in the field of arithmetic, I did not have the luxury of understanding concepts of plain arithmetic then. Even today, I sometimes get challenged, but I am a far cry from the days while sitting at the country kitchen table with my father. He eventually lost much of his patience with me.

    I envied kids sitting around me who immediately raised their hands to answer questions posed by the teacher. How they were able to hold all this information in their brains and have the confidence to answer the questions was mysterious to me. Learning, trying to comprehend mathematics and history was a major undertaking in junior and senior high school and college. These subjects made absolutely no sense to me even though I was studying. My parents did not know how to tutor us. They were just working hard to make ends meet. Because I failed Math Ten I had to stay back one year in high school and after taking Math Ten over three times, I finally passed. Many times my mother told me to go to my room and study. I would go there, but I would play with my dolls or sew something creative for them.

~*~

I was the only Jewish girl in my class in public school while in the lower grades. On one occasion our class learned Christmas carols, and there was a nativity scene in front of our classroom. Now this was public school. There was a Christmas pageant in which I took part and sang Christmas and German songs with the rest of the school choir. There was not anything that my father or mother could have done regarding this situation. My parents were not the type to rock the boat. They were still learning and understanding the proper American way of life. My parents were in their mid- thirties when they started having their family. For them being in a new country and learning the ropes of parenthood in their later ages, I am sure there was some adjustment and a learning curve for each one of them.

~*~

While attending a class in a lower grade in public school, I remember a thrilling experience. There were not many times as a youth that I would receive something pristinely new and something that was incredibly beautiful. We had a grab bag where we picked out someone's name to give a present to for the holidays. The student who picked my name gave me the most gorgeous handbag that to this day I still remember it. It was a brown drawstring leather-like bag with fringes and much beadwork. I felt exceptional using it, and it was something I was so proud to have. I felt like a queen. It was unusual to get something so chic and up to date. So often I would either get hand me downs or something that I did not like. This was certainly one exception.

~*~

An incident that was astonishing to me occurred when I was in the seventh grade while living in the country. I had a teacher for whom I had much respect, and I liked a great deal. While my mother was preparing dinner and setting the table beautifully for my birthday, she indicated that she had a surprise for me. What she was talking about, I had no idea. When it was just around the time for all of us to sit around the table, a car that was unfamiliar to me drove up our driveway. When a man came up to our front door, I found myself feeling embarrassed. It was none other than my teacher, Mr. Smith, whom I liked. How and why my mother would even have the slightest thought of inviting him is still beyond me. But she knew that I had lots of respect and caring for this teacher. The rest of the evening was fun, and we all enjoyed delicious food and a delectable chocolate birthday cake my mother had prepared.

During the evening I opened birthday gifts. I received some beautiful underwear from my aunt who worked for Lord & Taylor in New York City. These gifts were feminine and pretty, gifts I never expected to receive and were items that my mother would never have purchased for me even if she did have the money. She wanted me to stay naive. I quickly hid and put all these articles underneath other gifts that I received so that my teacher would not see them. After all, he was my teacher. I felt so embarrassed that he was even there to celebrate my birthday with my family and me. I remember feeling awkward and embarrassed seeing him in school thereafter.

~*~

Just having moved into the city of Albany, New York, in ninth grade, exposed me to many different types of situations than those that I was accustomed to while living in the country. One example was school. I attended Hackett Junior High School, named after the sixty-seventh mayor of Albany. It had a much broader ethnic and religious base than I was accustomed. Our class was on the first floor of a two-story building. There was this one tall, lanky boy who used to jump out the window of our room. That behavior distracted us, to say the least, and would then upset our teacher even more. This was our homeroom, and I found the situation rather unusual yet funny. As I think back on this circumstance at this moment it makes me laugh, actually. This teacher would get agitated and would yell at our whole class even more, and the students would not respect her even more and would often talk back to her. This kind of behavior was not only hysterical and exciting, coming from the perspective of my home life and type of school I came from, but also a totally new way of looking at a school atmosphere. There were some behavior problems that were an usual occurrence, something I was not accustomed to seeing. I was not used to hearing kids talk back to their teachers, and teachers yelling at kids, let alone kids jumping out of windows. Once school was let out, most everyone would run out as quickly as possible to go to their prospective homes, extracurricular activities, or hang out on the street or in the park.

One school day afternoon, I saw many kids running towards the park that was located around the corner of the school. I was still shy, quiet, and naive. Of what was happening in or about the dating scene, I had no idea. As I approached the park when everyone else was going there, I noticed two girls yelling and starting to fight with one another. Eventually these two girls were ripping each other's blouses off. They were fighting over a boy I was told. How liking a boy could have escalated into such activity, I could not imagine. Eventually everyone dispersed before the cops came and this was my introduction into city schools, interactions among one another, jealousy and fighting. This experience was thoroughly remarkable to me in that liking a boy would lead to such action by these two gals. That jealousy played a big part in this scuffle I would later on learn.

~*~

When my girlfriends and I were in high school, we walked everywhere and I mean everywhere. When all of us were walking together as a group one day, I remember we went past a fellow's home. Of course he had no idea that we were walking past his home. While walking with my friends, I had a feeling that I wished that I had a boyfriend and I wanted this, but I did not know how to accomplish it. My mother under no circumstances would have allowed me to have a boyfriend, anyway. She would not have approved of this under any condition.

These thoughts I kept a secret while walking past his home. Maybe, I hoped, just maybe, he would take notice of me. That certainly did not materialize, of course, but it was somewhat fun to fantasize about and at the same time, it became embarrassing. That there was hope this would ever even happen (when I reminisce about this now) certainly was ridiculous. But being a teenager, one has these visions, thoughts and hopes anyway; that is being a teenager!

Another time when I was hitchhiking in the city of Albany, three girlfriends and I hailed a car and jumped in. The car was new and we felt safe. I sat in the front seat and the rest hopped in the back. The man asked us where we wanted to go and we said in unison, "Just a few blocks up." Then I got a slight tap on my left shoulder from one gal, and she pointed to some wicked magazines that were on the seat next to her. Just then we decided to jump out of this car at the next light as fast as we could.

~*~

I am in the eleventh grade sitting in the guidance counselor's tiny little office. I am asked, "What would you like to do in the future after you leave high school?" She might as well have asked me if I can fly backwards. I had absolutely no idea what she was talking about. While I was growing up my mother or father never talked about what I was going to do or be in the future or what I was supposed to achieve in my later life after graduating from high school, never. At home there was not even any causal talk about this. Talk about being baffled. After graduating from high school, I had absolutely no idea what I was supposed to be doing or what I as supposed be.

~*~

During my teenage years, my mother wanted me to volunteer and help others. She may have felt that perhaps I would not focus on boys. I can still hear her say, "Any interest in boys is for after you graduate from high school." While I did not date in junior or senior high, many of my peers not only dated, but also in some cases, they were already having boyfriends and going steady. Since I was shy, I did not know how to relate to boys and felt too self-conscious to speak to them. I wanted what my peers had, and I did not want to feel left out and wanted to fit in. I was what you call a late bloomer. I found it difficult to express my feelings and myself, and how I was observing life around me. I had few clues on what was happening socially and conversing with my peers was difficult. When I once had a crush on a particular boy, I did not know how to act around him. I thought that if I looked into his eyes while speaking to him, he could tell that I liked him. This would have been too embarrassing, because I did not want him to know that I cared for him. It was just too uncomfortable and also, I knew, if my mother had any inkling of this she would have gone through the roof.

~*~

The only prom I ever attended was during my senior year of high school, and it was a novel and extraordinary experience. My mother made my strapless gown of beautiful light blue taffeta, mid-calf length, that looked store bought, and I bought light blue satin high heels. The dress was breathtaking, and it was unbelievable that she made such a beautiful garment. I felt good about myself, since I felt pretty, and yet I felt strange being in this kind of environment and situation. It was all so new to me. I was really nervous; was I saying and doing the right things? I did not want to make any social faux pas. I had a crush on the fellow that took me, and we double dated with my girlfriend and her date.

My experience with drinking was limited, and I had an inadequate experience of going out with a boy on a date. Other than drinking alcohol at religious holidays in my home, I did not drink. Drinking was not a big part of what my immediate family did. My father would have one beer on a Thursday evening when he arrived home late from working at his store all day, whereas my mother sipped her one drink, and she did not like the feeling she got that came from that drink. After my date and I danced and socialized at the prom, we all went on to another place to dance. He asked me what I would like to drink, and I had absolutely no clue on how to respond. What I picked out from a list of what I thought were strange names, I chose a Singapore Sling that had a disgusting taste. The taste was powerful, and I knew I did not want to drink that again. Drinking something having a much sweeter and smoother taste is what I would want in the future.

~*~

When I graduated from high school, I was never able to understand why anyone would want to get married after they graduated, when they could have the opportunity to go out into the world, to do whatever they want. Doing whatever one wanted to do without having one's parents interfere with them, this to me was real freedom. Growing up I had no options at all. I looked forward to the time when I would be able to do what, when and how I wanted. Not that I wanted or would have wanted to do anything to embarrass my family name, but just to be able to live easily and experience life without criticism, judgment and barriers. It is important for a child to grow up getting to make decisions on his or her own. Critical thinking and evaluating can then be learned. I did not experience this kind of upbringing.

# Employment

Not being an idle person, I read the daily newspaper that our family subscribed to, looking for some type of employment. I did not have the slightest idea for what I was looking. Something did jump out at me. In an advertisement, a bank was looking for people to run IBM proof machines in the transit department, the bank's clearinghouse, in Albany. I felt a bank would be a stable place to work. I apply, I get accepted, so right out of high school, for two full years, I am pounding down on keys of an IBM proof machine, with twenty-one other women, in what I would like to call doing menial labor. It was a means to an end of having the chance to start saving money so that I could eventually attend a college in the future or just for plain good old living.

One day while I am sitting at this job, toward the end of my two-year stint, bored no end and feeling as though I was going to have a nervous breakdown, I could stand it no longer. I said to myself, I quit! I got up off my chair, asked my supervisor if I could leave for a few minutes, went to the personnel department and took the risk of finally quitting a job that left me bored every day. Of course when I was initially accepted in doing this work, my mother seemed happy that I would now be working. Today I look back thinking, what the hell was this woman thinking? She seemed overjoyed that I was working at this bank. That our family did not have the financial means to send any one of us children to go on and further our education at a college, I knew. But, in this work atmosphere I was bored stiff doing the same task day in and day out, the same thing over and over again, banging my fingertips on those keys of the machine. It was utter monotony.

I could not relate to most of the women that were working there. There was only one gal with whom I was able to relate to out of the twenty-one gals. On our breaks in the morning, afternoon and at lunchtime, my peers usually talked, flirted with the guys working there, and gossiped about everybody. During our break there were a few who smoked cigarettes. In those days there were no limitations on smoking in public and private spaces. It was horrible to have to put up with the odor of cigarettes or even cigars. To be able to run off at lunchtime by taking long walks around the block gave me fresh air and some respite moments of peace and comfort.

Working at this task of continuously pounding on these keys all day long felt as though I were a robot. I was ready to jump out of my skin. The boredom eventually got to me. In fact, I wanted to make errors on these machines just to have something different happen once in a while. All day every day, I punched in amounts of the checks that had to be tallied and cleared, and then I had to prove out at the end of the day. The women doing these tasks the fastest were considered the "apple of their eye" to their managers. I was totally bored with all this mindless, rote work. After I quit I went on to college to get some real education. Of course, this too was a challenge for me because I was so lost. While sitting in my psychology classes, I felt as though I suffered from every possible kind of malady stated on all those white pages of the psychology books. It all sounded so feasible to me. Maybe I did not receive enough positive influence from my father while growing up, or maybe I needed to mature, or maybe all the losses that were in my family had an effect upon me! In any case, when I attended college, I was totally lost. I could not retain information or memorize what I was supposed to read and understand what I was reading. My anxiety level was high; I understand that now. After a few years, I quit that too and went on to work in the stockbrokerage business as an administrative assistant.

~*~

As I have already said, my main concern was to be able to make enough money to live on, due to not having come from a family that was heavily endowed financially. Not having the financial means to do the things that I wanted to do as a child and adolescent, I was aware that I had to work hard to make it. I would not give up until I earned enough of a salary that would sustain me. It was also very important that I live without having to rely on anyone else. Hence, the independent me!

My big break came one day when I finally landed a job I loved. This is how it went. On my way to my third and hopefully last job interview as a territory sales representative for Warner-Lambert Company, I was excited and understandably a bit nervous; I would now hopefully get my big break. The interviews were intense and grueling. The countdown was down to two people, a man and me. I was picked. I was the winner! That I was already a successful OEM (Original Equipment Manufacturer) sales representative with another firm was probably relevant in choosing me although I had not yet finished my college degree. In that sales position, it was seldom that a female would be hired. I was one of the first to hold that distinction. Feeling rather proud I was selected, I also felt elated that I would be working for this Fortune 500 Company and that this juncture in my life would give me the impetus to accumulate a nest egg for my future. The company had a great employee benefits package that included a company car, full health and dental insurance benefits and a two weeks' paid vacation. This job distinguished me as being able to come up to the plate, and I finally hit a home run and was accepted. I was thrilled of course.

On my way home from working with customers, I passed a car dealership and I was envious of this one car I had seen. I had made some extra money selling "off car" (selling product off of the car, which is sales jargon meaning I was allowed to sell product from my automobile). I felt that this purchase would work, and so I made the plunge to buy it. So now I had the luxury of not one car but of having two cars- a company car and a brand new one! Talk about extravaganza! Even though I had an extensive territory, excelled in sales, and won peer group contests, I became bored with the kind of work I was doing; it felt monotonous and unchallenging, too easy, and I started to lose interest in my job. I felt a change coming.

I was not brought up to be adventuresome in business, and surely not to take over my father's retail store or learn the rudiments of working in a store for that matter. One day I decided that with the many business contacts I already had, knowledge of marketing and sales that I had cultivated, and all my other accomplishments, I would now try my hand running my own business. I wrote a letter of resignation to my immediate supervisor giving him my two weeks' notice and then telephoned him to let him know of my plans on leaving the company. On the other end of the telephone, I heard the astonishment in his voice and he asked, "Is this a joke?" A joke it was not!

~*~

When I worked at my various jobs, I always looked forward to my vacations that usually involved a beach, surf and warm climate to places like Florida, or St. Maarten. Around March I would take two weeks off. I looked forward throughout the whole year to this welcomed respite. I would focus on these trips to keep me going with the usually boring and unchallenging jobs that I had. If it were not for these breaks in my work, I do not think that I would have been able to go on, because in many instances, I hated what I was doing. I liked very few jobs that I had.

I could not wait to finally be in my room, quickly change into a bathing suit and go to the beach. It was divine and one time I got such a burn because I stayed out too long in the afternoon, not having been in such a warm climate and not having sun block. There were a few times I sat with baby oil and iodine to make my tan faster and better! I liked that a tan would cover my varicose veins, which I was rather self-conscious about.

~*~

When it came to running my own business, which I excelled in, I liked the challenges of purchasing product for my customers. I managed my own wholesale business, selling toys, and varied impulse products to small and large mom and pop stores. My business also focused on creating and making high-end hair barrettes. When I told my mother about this new adventure of mine, she said, "When are you going to have a real job?" It crushed me what she said. I remember clearly saying under my breath something not nice; it was around the Thanksgiving dinner table, with her sitting almost directly across from me.

Some of the gifts that I got from working for myself is that I enjoyed very much setting up my own schedule on where to go and what customers to see. With the many business contacts I had acquired, I felt that that this new challenge in my life would work out well. I liked working at my own company. It was worth taking this major risk of leaving a decent job and I did well.

# College

I attended Junior College of Albany and took a class in Speech. Left to my own devices, I never would have picked this subject to study in a million years. Even though it was required for my Liberal Arts Degree, I was not enthused in taking it. It was now or never. The thought of getting up in front of the class to speak, made me feel so scared; I shudder at the thought of how I felt, even now. I did not have the confidence whatsoever at that time to speak in front of a group and did not know how I was going to talk in front of this class. We all had the chance to practice, yet I just did not get any better; and when I stood in front of my peers, my mind went completely blank. Even when I would share on a topic that I knew, it did not get any better. It was a painful, humiliating experience.

Now for the final grade, I needed to find a topic to speak on, and I was even allowed to have information put on a four by six-inch index card for reference while speaking. I walked up to the front of the class, stood there for a moment and may have uttered one or two words, and then all of a sudden I turned around and headed right back to my seat. I still remember that horrible feeling of embarrassment that I had of not being able to accomplish speaking in front of my class, and of not receiving a passing grade. I felt dreadful and stupid at the time and got a "D" in speech class.

Today I have come a long way in that I sometimes speak in front of groups about what happened. For just a minute or two, I still get a slight tinge of fear although that eventually dissipates.

~*~

Much later in my adult life I was finally awarded my Bachelor of Arts degree that I started many years prior, forty-five years to be exact. For years I have wanted to finish what I had originally started out to do in college, to get a degree. Applying myself in the world of academia had not been something I was able to do; I just did not know how.

My wish to finally complete my degree was a huge effort; I finally came through this time and with a vengeance! It almost seemed effortless; it was such an exciting experience. Majoring in psychology with an emphasis in human development and a minor in art, I carried a 4.0 and in the majority of my classes, even received an A-plus as my final grade. This achievement has thrilled me to no end. It was something I was unable to accomplish in prior years. There is a saying, "When the student is ready, a teacher will appear." And not only one but also many! Again, this thread in my life of being a late bloomer still continued. This most recent experience of going back to college was most enjoyable, educational, inspiring and monumental. Not only did I have stimulating and exceptional mentors, but also I had an exceptional thirst for learning, to excel and finally get that degree that I have always sought. Receiving it was a wonderful achievement that I did for myself and no one else. I was determined.

During this time in college I gained a thirst for reading and writing papers in my classes. Finally understanding and learning how to write opened up a brand new door for me. I expressed myself in a manner I could not do before, by creating artwork out of words and by fashioning sentences by putting these words down on paper. This process felt creative, like formulating artwork; but this was a form so different than creating my art in that I was a building a sentence from words instead of building my art using paint or found objects. Art and writing are a passion of mine to this day, even though each one consists of a different form of creative process.

~*~

Restless as I was I never could just sit still for a while, not even a smidgeon, to read a book like my sister, who would stay at home and sit for hours reading. Not only was it difficult to try to understand the written word, but also to sit for hours and then try to absorb what the author was attempting to say. This was foreign and impossible for me. I envied my sister to no end and wondered how she was able to do that. In fact it baffled me.

I now understand and know and am able to appreciate the written word and what one is trying to convey on paper. I only had to wait for my time and my time has been now. Finally! Hooray!

Memoir of a 2G

# Leaving Home

Leaving home for the first time, I felt frightened, frightened that I might be unable to survive. After all, until the point of leaving, I always had a warm bed to come home to, food on the table and a secure environment in which to live. So when I stop to think just for a moment where I came from financially and spiritually, I am completely astounded.

Remembering that one room that I initially rented and lived in, having had only one bathroom down the hall that I shared with others on that second floor is reminiscent of how far I have come in my life. By today's standards, it was small, needed some new paint on the walls and had limited light from the outside. The huge red brick building was built in the nineteen thirties and was on a busy street across from a big park, with easy access to different stores, libraries and schools. The building had a musty smell with dark halls and had been split up into many apartments and rooms that were rented out. To add some color to make my place more habitable, I purchased a package of colored construction paper and put different colored pieces of paper up on the wall to make it a bit more elegant. It looked odd at first, but I was able to get used to this kind of interior decorating due to my lack of funds; it had to suffice at the time. I had no other options.

As the saying goes, "I have come a long way baby!" The opportunities that I have had to further my education, get the jobs that I got, I have traveled, attain friendships and just be able to get on with ordinary life, is remarkable. With much perseverance, consistency, drive and type-A personality, I have been able to achieve a nice lifestyle. Other children had more money, were prettier, and had a bigger home, a newer car, a boyfriend, much better school marks, and the list goes on. Initially I thought and felt I was a loser. Over time I eventually ceased to compare myself with others. I just did the next right thing, put one foot in front of the other and believed I would come to a better place. Boy, is that the truth. I was bewildered at first. But I carried on.

I questioned the presence of a being or a spirit bigger than me. Confusion about horrible circumstances and outcomes did not constitute a place for a spirit. I now have some ability to understand that God did not do bad things. I am now better able to view that it was the human race that did such horrific things whether within families, friends, wars or in a group. Eventually, I was able to comprehend this new piece of information. It was not until then that I was able to go forward with my life on a daily basis and with a great deal of peace and a new set of eyes to view the world we live in.

~*~

Not only did I move around a bit while growing up, but also I would continue this pattern of moving from place to place while living on my own. As years passed, whenever I moved I would get better lodgings, having lived initially frugally and for many years thereafter. I just took that leap, that risk. It was now or never. It was an action I felt that I needed to do, to go forward with my life. I relied upon my intuition but with much fear. I left home in search of my own true identity of who I am, to be myself and become extroverted.

~*~

Since I worked hard, put money away for rent and saved for the future, I was eventually able to purchase a place of my own. It was a two-story building with two apartments in a city; I lived upstairs while I rented the apartment beneath me. What would happen if I could not pay the mortgage or what would happen if I had problems with tenants or what would happen if the place needed something fixed that broke? I had some trepidation because this was my first endeavor in real estate. All these things went through my mind, but I knew that I had to start somewhere and just go through with this fear and it would all work out. And so that is exactly what I did. I took the plunge. Saving and investing for my future, I thought this would be a good investment, a good start for my life.

Owning property certainly had its challenges, but when rent payment was due and I received rent payment from a tenant, this would somewhat minimize the problems that had ensued that previous month. The tenant was jealous of me because I was a woman who owned my own real estate. It was customary for men to dominate the real estate business where I lived and renters were usually accustomed to dealing only with men. They were unaccustomed to dealing with a woman. This experience stepped me up to the plate, and I had some remarkable results. On one occasion, I rented to an older woman and when she finally left, I needed to make the decision to keep her security deposit because of the way the apartment was left when she left; it was dirty and the stove and oven were abominable with grit. I was cordial and kind to this person while she resided there and would even ask her on a few occasions if she needed anything from the grocery store. When she finally left and no longer rented from me, her relatives called me some nasty names when I would not return her security deposit.

# Love

Finally, I got my first boyfriend at the age of twenty-one. After not having been allowed to date while attending junior or senior high school, this was a really big deal. Having met him at the college we attended, I was enamored by how smart he was, his ability to get all A's in classes, his good looks, his acting abilities and his knowledge on how to act in a group and be so self-confident. For seven years I dated this guy. As I got to know him better or so I thought, there were flaws in his personality that I did not like, but being impressed on how he was so smart that he got all A's and how well liked he was by his peers, something overcame me; I was unable to let go of this relationship. He may have been smart, but he was prejudiced. I just hung on because I did not know how to get out of it.

On Saturday evenings we got together and he used to pick me up where I lived and then take me over to his parents' home, where he lived. Eventually I learned how to cook with an Italian flair because his mother was of Italian heritage. On a rare occasion, his father said that even though I was Jewish, I seemed different. Not until much later in our relationship I heard my boyfriend say something derogatory about Jews, and he too said something about my being different. The apple does not fall far from the tree! Again, because I did not know how to debate or say something to the contrary, I had no comeback to what I heard from either one of them. After a lovely dinner that his mother prepared, he and I would then go visit one of his close friends who was much older than we, and we would all play pinochle. I learned the game and got the gist of it. While playing I heard derogatory remarks about certain groups made by his friend and my boyfriend, and they would just laugh it off and I would feel horrible. But again I did not know how to respond to what was being said. Wait a minute, he is talking about me! I froze. I did not know how to respond to the vitriol that was spewing from his lips. And in other ways, he was arrogant in the way he spoke. In a way, I became numb, scared and just played on as though nothing happened or that what they were saying had no significance to me or hoped that these feelings would just go away. This feeling would come over me until I just wanted to run out of that house. I felt embarrassed and scared by what I was hearing about blacks and Jews.

A situation such as this one made me realize that I did not want to be with this guy, but I did not know how to get out of this relationship. Even though I wanted to, I could not make that move. Later my boyfriend's number came up in the lottery, and he was drafted into the army. I felt the freedom of a reprieve and safety of being able to do what I wanted. Even though I wanted to be loyal to him, I did not want anything to do with him. Eventually I stopped writing to him and felt scared of the time when he would eventually come home. There was awkwardness when he came back to the States, and I saw him and I do not know what I said, I only knew it was over and thankfully so. That his mother taught me a few things about cooking and that she was nice to me balanced out some of the negative experiences that occurred throughout my relationship with him, and that she took the time to teach me the rudiments of cooking I will always be appreciative. Too, I am grateful that I never married this guy, even though I spent seven years of my life dating him.

~*~

I eventually fell in love with another man; I was crazy in love with him. As I look back to those years, the thought of losing my freedom to do what I wanted when I wanted, kept me from making a permanent commitment forever. The thought of love was ecstatic, but the thought of losing my autonomy would have its costs. So, I never married this man even though he and I were in a committed relationship. These seven years were filled with highs and lows. To this day I have a heavy heart and a love I never encountered with anyone else. Those good memories are a gift today in that I am capable of remembering, reminiscences of running, biking, walking in the rain, having dinners together and more. I was in a quagmire; I wanted this love, yet was overridden with anxiety and had some good ole American living to do. I dreaded giving up my independence; I wanted to be as free as a bird, to do what I wanted, when I wanted, without any interference by anyone saying no.

~*~

Growing up I did not experience many couples and families around me; I did not get the occasion to view how people got along and how they communicated with one another. My point of reference was bickering, arguing and yelling. I was unsure of what qualities to look for in a partner. Looks, humor, and intelligence were the qualities I chose in a partner. Of course, they alone are not enough for a bubbling and successful relationship. Charming and smart do not cut the mustard. All other aspects of a person's behavior and thoughts come with that package. I did not know what I was doing, which certainly added much fuel to the already set fire. I thought that all other people had those behaviors happening to them in their lives. The behaviors certainly were not the best attributes to bring into any relationship. On the other end of the spectrum- mild and meek did not work either.

~*~

While traveling on the subway one afternoon on my way to Brighton Beach in Brooklyn, sitting directly across from me, I noticed a father who was very attentive to his three children. I found myself staring, and I could not take my eyes off of him and his children. It was beautiful to watch and I realized the void that I had of not having my father's presence emotionally, not having the proper nurturing and having a lack of demonstrative love. I kept watching this father, who was soft spoken and acted kindly toward his children. This behavior was all foreign to me, even as I, an adult, was sitting there. I was in awe and was mesmerized because seldom, if ever, did I witness this kind of affection or attention in my home by either one of my parents.

# Travel

Singapore was a destination that I wanted to visit. It seemed like an alluring city, modern and advanced. The brochures divulged an enthralling and appealing place to me with all its progressive modern architecture, gorgeous flora, and warm and tropical weather. As I was preparing for this journey, I had the opportunity of staying with a couple whom I was friends with since junior high school. I took this trip by being a courier because it was an inexpensive way to see the world. The courier company gave me a sealed, large envelope, the kind an attorney might use, and once I handed it over to the correct party, I was able to spend the rest of the weeks to travel and sightsee all I wanted.

When my plane arrived at the Tokyo Airport, I was to give this package to a person who would greet me. These were the days with no mobile phones, before Homeland Security, let alone any other types of computer generated private information. I had no idea what person I was to look for, nor had I any knowledge of the Japanese language. As I got off the plane at the airport in Tokyo, the stewardess told me to be back within twenty to thirty minutes to continue on to my final destination, Singapore.

Standing by myself in this vast lobby in the airport upstairs, having hundreds of people running about to their prospective planes around me, holding on to a package given to me in New York, how was I to know whom to look for? I felt as though this was a form of foreign intrigue. Scurrying all around me were men, women, and children that gave me no clue to whom to hand over this package. After a few brief minutes, a Japanese man came up to me. He acknowledged me with barely a nod and no words were spoken. We eyed one another, I handed him the envelope, and I went back on the plane. How he knew I was the person caring the envelope, I to this day have not a clue. The courier company had no picture of me. How did this man know? And as I was not the only non-Asian female standing around in this lobby, I always wondered if in fact this was the correct person with whom I was to have made that encounter. After I got back on to the plane, I continued on to Singapore.

The experiences that I encountered going to Raffles, an exceptional Hotel with its gorgeous architecture and columns, extensive history, incredibly modern shopping malls, Little India with its delicious food, Chinatown, gorgeous horse racetrack, were enormous and thrilling. My three weeks were encompassed with joy and excitement. My hosts went out of their way to make sure that I had one of the best of times outside the United States.

~*~

In the past I have not ever wanted to travel to Germany because of what happened to my family as well as what happened to other people of that era. Whenever I meet someone with a heavy German accent, I wonder if they were Jewish, and if they were not, I questioned where might their soul be or where they may have come from, and especially whether they or their ancestors were involved with the Nazi regime.

# Art

My imagination has led me on a path of art and creativity that has been witty, fun and inspiring. Throughout part of my life if I was not constructing doll clothing for my dolls, I was picking wild flowers from all the vast beautiful meadows where we resided in the country, creating my own clothing, drawing and painting. Some years after graduating from high school, I had an idea to investigate and start the process of filling out forms to attend the Rochester Institute of Technology, known for its art program. Having been accepted by their admissions committee, I still had to fill out the rest of the application, writing out the essay portion of why I picked this school. I did not feel confident enough, intellectually and monetarily. I did not have a clear vision of what I was supposed to write about, nor did I have a clue on how to write down on paper my ideas, feelings and thoughts. I felt I was a bit unsure and incapable of going to this college and certainly not smart enough to attend. Therefore, I did not conclude the process and finally gave up. Maybe it was just not my time. There have been a few moments later on when I have sometimes wondered if I could have made it at that college.

~*~

When I was in my twenties, riding my Fiji ten-speed bicycle around for thirty miles, I remember seeing on the side of the road a gorgeous example of a large flat piece of rust. Since I was twenty-five miles from home, carrying it on my back on the return trip was not an option. There was something that caught my eye, the patina, the natural beauty and texture that was just perfect. I am today still enamored by rust or what I call weathered metal.

Today this is what I do- I get absolutely delighted scavenging at a dump or wash in the Sonoran desert looking for weather-beaten metal with its beautiful shapes, objects from which to create my next piece of art from. I also look for rusty metal by the road, and use it for the art I produce. The scruffier the piece of metal that I find, the better I feel!!

~*~

In my earlier mixed media days, I used many found objects that I gathered; leaves, bark, metal, feathers, paper, bean pods, etc. I made a big piece of art on canvas that was beautiful, incorporating leaves, paper, and bean pods from a mesquite tree on the right side of the art piece. When I finished, I hung it on my art room wall. While working in that room, I occasionally heard a crackling sound, although nothing caught my eye where this might be coming from. Another time that similar sound of a light popping and crackling came again. I finally came to realize that it was coming from this art piece where I had incorporated the many bean pods. And guess what I found out? Upon closer inspection I saw there were holes in the beans and bruchid beetles were trying to get out. I was flabbergasted. I disassembled the art piece immediately, took all the bean pods off because I knew it was only a matter of time when this artwork would disintegrate.

I learned from this experience that when I pick out found objects, I better be sure they are devoid of any living organisms.

~*~

In later years I became an arts and crafts teacher, then arts and crafts director, and much later I became an artist as well as an art teacher. When I was finally finishing up my college degree, I was praised by my art professor on the various types of art that I produced in his class. That my fourth grade teacher was able to recognize my talent and understand this about me when I was only in the fourth grade was perceptive, and revealing on her part. She was right on!

~*~

Most recently I have had three art exhibits in the Southwest displaying my artwork. They have been an achievement. In the first one, I sold my first piece of art. There is a satisfaction I receive from sharing my creativity with the public. Not until recently have I turned to painting even though assemblage, mixed media and working with found objects are still passions of mine. It has been an adventure not only to produce art but also to put into fruition the process of setting up a show that is a particularly tedious and challenging undertaking. When attending open art studios, museums and galleries, I have a better knowledge of the intricacies of hanging an art show because of my own experience. I now have a totally different and new perspective as well as respect for the whole process.

~*~

Although I never had children of my own, I have had many opportunities to be around and teach them by being an arts and crafts teacher in the afternoons at a community center, and babysitting for families during the week and weekends. During summers in high school, I taught arts and crafts at a day camp for teenagers. Working with children has been a joy in my life. Having had the challenge of teaching art and helping children discover their creative side has been a rewarding experience. The kids have been given an opportunity to express themselves through the process of art instruction, and they have created gorgeous artwork. One just has to give them the break, time and space to do so.

Of late I taught art to teenagers in Marana Middle School in Arizona in an after school setting. This class was from a grant the school was able to get. The kids created exceptional artwork, and I sense that they looked forward to getting together every week. I have been able to pass on to them what I have learned. I set up a curriculum and incorporated various media, paint, found objects, collage and more that the kids had the opportunity to use. I only wish there were more time to accomplish making more art. The creativity and growth they have been able to achieve have been wonderful to observe.

# Fear

In my family, I was responsible for babysitting and watching over my two younger brothers and sister. As a young girl, I had few skills and sometimes became firm towards my siblings during those periods; I was the older sister and yet was at a young age myself.

One occasion related to this sticks out vividly in my memory because it became scary. I was babysitting for my youngest brother when we were living in the country. With no immediate neighbors of any kind to turn to, my brother, who was three, came to me crying when he got his index finger caught and stuck between the top lid and bottom part of a tuna can that he found in the wastebasket. He would lose the tip of his finger if I erred, and I had to make a quick decision on what to do. If I pulled his finger out, I would slice the tip of his finger off and if I pushed the top of the can lid further in, that too would slice his fingertip off. How I ever got his tiny finger out of that dilemma even today surprises me. But by a miracle, I was able to spare his finger, thank goodness. Some of these situations made me a better solution-oriented girl even at the ripe young age of fourteen. The experiences that I encountered early on in my life aided me to come up with the best possible solutions for me then and certainly now.

~*~

When I lived in the country at the time I was around seven or eight years old, I had some fears because of some strange occurrences near my home.

While walking on the main dirt road adjacent to our home, having the warm summer sun basking upon me, I found a brown crumpled paper bag with a dead kitten in it. How it got there was a total mystery to me. My mother told me that the kitten had been chloroformed. As a young kid I had never heard that word spoken, and it sounded rather gruesome. She tried to explain to me in the best way possible without scaring me that some people just were not nice.

~*~

One late warm summer evening, I looked out of my cozy upstairs bedroom window after I woke up, and I saw a fire roaring out of control at the end of our long driveway that led from the end of the main dirt road to our home. Talk about something unusual and scary! My parents told me a neighbor's car got on fire. To this day, I still am unable to figure out how that situation occurred. What I do remember is the fear I had thinking that this roaring orangey-red fire in the late evening would come up the driveway and engulf our home. Oh, the imagination of a child!

~*~

One time my mother was telling her friend's fortune at my house. She had two sons. One time this friend's one son came with her to my home. He took me for a drive in his car, and he and I ended up on a secluded country road at a creek and we sat there for a while. It was surprising and interesting that my mother would allow me to be with him alone, because she was so protective of me. I was in my early teens. While he and I were sitting on the ground, he was sitting in a way as to expose himself. I thought I would die! I had never been at this young age in this sort of compromising situation before. Being shocked at what I saw, I could not believe this situation was happening. I was unable to express my astonishment and I was scared. My immediate reaction was, and I said to him, "I want to go home." He obliged and I never told my father or mother or anyone else what transpired that afternoon. While sitting there with him, he knew he was exposing himself, I know that now. Aware that I was a shy and quiet kid with no experience being around other males outside of my home, he thought that he could do this. He was taking advantage of my naiveté, and he felt that I would not tell anyone about this incident. And if that is what he was surmising, he was correct. Not until now I have told anyone and now I am telling the world, and it feels good. I did find him a bit strange thereafter. That nothing further occurred regarding that situation, I am so grateful. What a jerk! Typically many stories similar to this one do not end up with such a good ending, I know that now.

~*~

In my senior high school, I used to teach arts and crafts to teenagers in an after school program at a community center. Everywhere I went I walked. On one such occasion, while I was walking to this center, a man driving a car approached me. He was the husband of a girlfriend's friend. He asked, "Would you like a ride to the center?" I said, "Yes." He proceeded to explain and give me an answer to something that perplexed me often. It was about a situation that I was going through every Monday evening around six o'clock. There were telephone calls that I used to get, I said hello, and this person said nothing. Upon hearing nothing, I would immediately hang up. I was not so much scared as annoyed. This went on for a while and I wondered who the person was and why anyone would behave like this. I had no term for that kind of behavior or idea that this man was stalking me. What I learned since is that someone who is repeatedly calling a home or work is called a stalker.

As I am sitting in this man's car, he starts to explain to me that he has been the person calling on the telephone when I would hang up. Upon hearing all this, I was shocked. So now I am in the car of a man who has possibly been stalking me and calling and hanging up! Now I was scared! He then proceeded to tell me if I wanted to tell the authorities on him, he would understand. Still in shock, I said I would not, and then he left me at the center. And thank goodness nothing more happened.

Finally, I was relieved to find out who this jerk was who was harassing me with all those phone calls, but then astonished to find out he was the husband of one of my girlfriend's friends. Thereafter, I told no one. He was a weird guy, and I felt I wanted to stay clear of him. This same person I would notice roaming around in the park with his camera near where I lived. Today I am convinced that he was probably not taking pictures of any flowers in the park! I am grateful that nothing more occurred and that I handled the situation with grace by not overreacting.

~*~

When I was older, old enough to drive and still living at home in the city, my sister and I took a road trip by car to visit someone in Kentucky. This trip occurred after the time my father died. My mother was left with a Studebaker Lark car that no one in the family could drive because no one had a driver's license. I practiced how to drive using this car and finally received my official New York State driver's license. The first time I failed the driving test because when I approached the *Stop* sign the examiner said, "You can go right through!" And of course, I did go right through! The second time I passed.

After our pleasant visit to Kentucky, we started driving back home to New York. While traveling on a road going back home, all of a sudden I heard a large thump sound and realized that I had hit the car ahead of us ever so lightly. Immediately frightened by what might occur next, I was also scared of the damages that may have happened not only to my mother's car but also what would happen to us, now that we were in another state far away from home. This man got out of his car, looked over the details and he assessed that there were not enough damages to warrant contacting the police. I got out of our car and looked at what possible damage I may have caused not only to his car but also to ours. With no visible damage done to either one of our vehicles, I felt a bit relieved that I had hit his car fender ever so lightly. He was a kind gentleman with a quiet demeanor. He happened to be a minister! How fortunate! And what luck! I was grateful for such positive results. No police, no mark on my license and no damage to either one of our cars! My sister and I continued on our journey home and with no further mishaps. Hooray!

## New York City

Wishes do come true. When I was much younger, I traveled south down the New York State Thruway by bus and arrived at the Port Authority in Manhattan. It was a Wednesday late morning. I walked for seven hours including going to stores on 5th Avenue. As I headed home, I wished I could reside there. I got so caught up with the many sounds, sights, smells, and delicious foods that I sadly had to leave behind. I frequently traveled to Manhattan, with the want and hope to eventually live there. That wish has finally come true. Living bicoastal has awarded me the opportunity to experience life in the Southwest as well as in the Northeast. As one who has spent time in Manhattan can attest, there are so many varied, delightful and stimulating experiences to live by. Possibly, maybe, I am wandering alongside some similar paths and places my father and mother went to and reliving some of their experiences when they resided there. In any case, for someone who loves art, good food, music, dance, theater and nature, it is definitely a place second to none with so many great golden opportunities.

~*~

While growing up, I was exposed to opera and classical music. Rock 'n' roll or any other popular kind of music was out of the question to listen to freely. On

Sunday afternoons, we listened to music coming from Lincoln Center over FM radio station WQXR in our home. When I was much older and living on my own, I enjoyed different genres of music such as rock and roll, jazz, and soul music. Hearing all the passion that came from listening to these various types was exciting and soothing. I was enthralled with the melodies.

A captivating concert I attended a while ago at the Fillmore East in lower Manhattan featured the reggae master, Bob Marley. The tunes went right through me and the concert was incredible. Hearing him live and observing his outrageous energy energized the whole audience including me. It was spectacular and I was enthralled! The opportunities I had to attend various venues of music broadened my interest, enthusiasm and educated me. I went so far as to usher at Saratoga Performing Arts Center in Saratoga Springs, NY. I was truly captivated, not only by what I saw, but also by what I heard. Performances coming from James Taylor, Steve Miller and his band, Humble Pie, Chicago, and others were just a few examples of what I was gratefully able to hear.

Too, some of the places that I attended were a bit unsavory and yet the thrill of being there thrilled me immensely. After an establishment closed at the end of the night, I would then go to an after-hours place to hear jazz. All at once I felt scared and energized. It felt as though I was participating with the in- crowd and would enter through the main door on street level, and then proceed down a dark staircase into a smoke filled room. What happened in the other rooms in this basement, I did not understand and for that matter did not want to know. There was a pool table in one of the rooms. Most everyone looked out for everyone else. Having been a bit naïve, I certainly took a risk of attending some of these precarious places, but it was well worth every penny to hear some of the top music in jazz, soul, rhythm and blues.

Memoir of a 2G

## Southwest

A considerable time later on in my life, I received a telephone call from my sister who wanted to know if I would want to visit her in Arizona. Traveling is one of my passions, so if I am asked, I usually say, "Yes!" The Southwest was an entirely new territory for me, and I looked forward to this trip. Once I arrived in Tucson, I fell in love with its serenity and natural beauty. This type of beauty was second to none, especially around evening, with the sky showing many shades of pink, violet, and orange. Of course, the magnificent and majestic saguaro cactus stood tall in the Sonoran desert. It was breathtaking. Intuitively I had a feeling that I was supposed to move to this paradise. When I returned to the East Coast, I wanted to make sure I had the same feeling of yearning, and the answer was yes! I got a mover, put my home up for sale and journeyed on to the Southwest to experience a new form of existence. And I have not turned back.

In the southwest where I live, there are the most gorgeous colors coming from cacti. The tiny flowers of reds, pinks and yellows have the backdrop of the green from the cacti, and they are like they are on stage showing off their resilience, beauty and proudness and that they have made it through another hot day. Their colors are just glorious and luminous.

~*~

I continued attending flea markets and antique shops when I moved to the southwest. After speaking to a man several times at a flea market who was selling his possessions and collections, we became acquaintances. A few times on weekends, we went to garage sales. After a time of becoming acquainted, he invited me to his home to see the much talked about items he collected. Southwestern furniture was one of his joys or so I thought.

As he was showing me around from room to room in his medium sized one floor southwest style home, one room we entered made me freeze. As I stood there, I became numb, frightened, and was in total shock. My heart had palpitations. I did not know what to say. In front of me was a mannequin dressed in Nazi regalia. Alongside the mannequin were varied Nazi items. When I see a swastika insignia it usually does something to me. I want to avoid, not see and run away. In this situation I wanted to sprint! This man later on said he had never met a Jewish woman. He was a collector of Nazi items. It disturbed me so, that someone was making money on all this stuff. Knowing where my father and mother had come from and what their history was about, seeing this upset me significantly. I left this man's home with a heavy heart. I was unable to communicate and explain to him just how I felt; I was too scared and shocked. I wanted to get out of there as fast as possible. Understanding that these items were actually worn by Nazis gave me chills. I was shocked and felt helpless not ever having been in a situation such as this before. Who would ever want to have items such as these in their home, I thought? It was too close to home for me. I never went back to visit again. What an experience!

~*~

Today was a special day even though it did not come out the way I wanted it. Throughout my earlier life and later, I was told that my relatives were no longer living either due to the Holocaust or because of natural causes. But then a rabbi helped me retrieve one answer to some of my dreams. He helped me write a letter in English, and he translated the letter into Hebrew addressed to someone in Israel at an address that I found in some of my genealogy papers. He wanted to help determine that there was a cousin out there somewhere.

The letter with the name "Resident" on the envelope was sent to Israel through the United States Post Office. This same letter came back to me with an inscription "Unknown" stamped on the outside envelope. Again I sent it out, and it came back to me. I did not want to give up yet. For one last time I sent this letter out and researched a zip code that I felt finally was the correct one. Well! Finally, the day came when I received an answer by email and so did the rabbi. From the help of someone in Israel familiar with this address, I was given some important information so that I could contact a person residing in Iowa. This was a shot in the dark. I learned early on while doing genealogy research that one starts with what they know, do not assume anything, and take the next step to find out the answer.

Having been told that it is possible that this person could be a cousin of mine, I finally got in touch with him. The rabbi also called this man, and yes, this man is a cousin of mine who is in his eighties. Although he cares not to communicate further or befriend me, it is a good feeling there is someone out there who is related to my family and me. He is an emeritus professor with studies in mechanical engineering at a university in the United States. I am baffled, excited and sad, that after all these years, and I mean all these years, there is a person to whom I am related besides my siblings, but he suggested that I have no further contact with him, and I will honor his request.

# Philosophy

As a youth as well as into my adulthood I have frequently felt as though I could not relate to what was going on in the world around me. Not only had I often felt differently from my peers, but also thought in a different way because of my experiences and background. There were instances where I wanted to fit in but did not know how. I just felt awkward in social situations and with people I had contact with in ordinary everyday life. The skill to speak in certain ways so I would be able to fit in or have the correct retort just did not happen.

There have been situations where I have felt empathetic towards other peoples' situations. Sometimes I would have an awareness that I feel other people did not to have. There is no denying being the first-born child and brought up by Holocaust survivors has affected me in not the most positive way. My parents' trauma along with some of their survival experiences were certainly passed down, and I understand now what effect this had on how I thought and felt as a child; there is no question. I did not want to be who I was, neither my ethnicity nor my religion. Some people who recognized my differences were not kind. Along with being called bad names, some attempted to stereotype and categorize me and put me in a box. I was who I was; I cannot be somebody else, no matter how hard I might have wanted to be. I was not a light skinned, blue-eyed blonde girl that came from a middle class American family, that is all.

On the topic of stereotyping, I now recognize it was an experience and a big part of my growing up. My thinking and actions in enough instances were not similar to my peers. Let me give an example. There were many occasions when girls would speak about boys and dating. These situations made me feel strange and uncomfortable; I did not date in high school because my parents did not allow it, my discomfort of not fitting in was rather pronounced in that arena. For not knowing how to fit in, I was judged as awkward and shy. By not being accepted by some friends and a peer group was especially difficult in that I felt hurt or having a feeling of worthlessness because I was not one of them or that I did not act the way they acted. The interesting point today is that my uniqueness and even maybe my oddness I learned to deal with, and I want to be who I am today. This harsh lack of acceptance gave me the ability to become even stronger and eventually take on criticism without letting it hold me back.

~*~

Why some people want to be mean or distant and yet would like to be in a relationship, I cannot figure out. With regards to relationships, I am still somewhat baffled as to what constitutes a loving and caring relationship. Game playing and distancing that exists with some men are some examples that are interesting. So why does this actually happen and often happen? I have not been able to figure that one out at all. It has been a painful experience and yet exciting to date a guy and find out if there is in fact some compatibility between us. I told my spiritual guide that by the time I live at the old age home, and maybe by then, I will find a soul mate or someone who will want to be with me unconditionally, to share his love and compassion and not want to argue and be nasty.

That there is another more beneficial way to live and treat someone, I certainly did not understand. All this lack of knowledge of living played a part when I was younger. As an adult it has been a journey to meet a man who cares about himself, respects the environment, and then of course, me. My determination and strength have helped me to forge through and date, attempting just one more time to do this coupling thing.

My idealism started around 21 years of age. I remember I wanted to save the world in which we all lived, and I especially wanted people to be kind and care for one another. I was relatively aware of the skin color thing and the Jewish thing yet could never comprehend what occurred around prejudice then and today.

I was perplexed to the terms that there were "white people" and "colored people," while growing up. White is a color too and why all the fuss? For that matter, no one is actually black or actually white, but tones from those colors. Too, it puzzled me why advertisements were only with "white" people and not the shades of skin of people that were around me. It confused me so.

~*~

We live and then we die. Often I have wondered what our existence is all about. Sometimes I am unable to understand and have confusion about different facets of life. We sleep, eat, go to work, have hobbies, exercise, and help others. We are on this earth but for a short, a real short while, I am aware, and it still amazes me of how much I still do not know. Finding out how people communicate with their words, as I do with my art, is interesting to me, and fortunately I love to read and relish all the beauty in words. Even though I have friends that care and a life worth living, I still get confused on what this presence on earth is all about. I have some difficulty in understanding what some people think is so important in life, and I will not contribute to some of the pettiness that exists. I was taught by my parents, especially my mother, that there are some basic values that are important, and that I carry in living my life. They consist of the following: kindness, integrity, caring for those less fortunate, social justice, real relationships, taking care of the land and environment, and standing up for principles that are advantageous to one's society.

Simplicity and beauty are subjective; I appreciate having beauty surrounding me in nature, good people and a home that has a pleasant space. My house is my home. Visually I am capable of creating a pleasant space and even with a limited budget if necessary. When it comes to knowing what is important in life, I have few clues; I am still learning. It has been a slow process.

What is popular among a majority of people today, meaning the proliferation of new electronic innovations, has taken away the presence of what is going on at any given moment. Having some people attached to their electronic devices has affected their way of living. In some ways I feel that this obsession with electronics has robbed some people of the true meaning of life and the important insights to what better living ought to be. Communicating with one another, face-to-face has become limited and when we do communicate, it is over the Internet, VM and other electronic devices.

An interesting sight I experienced while I was walking down a street in Manhattan on a beautiful sunny Sunday, mid-morning; three young girls in their teens, well dressed in their finery, walking abreast all speaking not to one another, but each of them talking into their cell phones. It was somewhat comical to view in that here were three gals that had the option of speaking to one another and instead chose not to speak to one another! Too, they were not even noticing the beautiful day or even going window-shopping!

When I experience little children gathered together and see how many of them are on their cell phones, tablets, etc. it concerns and saddens me. Having direct eye contact is a thing of the past and good listening skills have gone out the window. Certainly communicating via all these new modes of chatting has its place.

~*~

As I grew older, I was obsessed by certain ideas of living, and became bossy to what needed to be accomplished. Until I came into my own, I wanted to be accurate in my behavior and attitude, chores done in an instant, and without any excuses. Perfection and immediacy were to be relished. This idea of perfectionism actually delayed and froze me from going forward in trying new things in my life because the thought of failing would have been too difficult to deal and live with. Wanting to do life in a thorough way paralyzed my efforts to, at times, not do anything at all.

~*~

As one gets older, isn't one supposed to get calmer, accept what has occurred, take the hand they were dealt and not "rock the boat"? The older I got or get, the more I have wanted to know and comprehend what is going on around me. This is being akin to putting a 500-piece picture puzzle together, as each piece gets closer to the fuller picture, there is a filled and keen eye of completeness.

It has taken much time, traveling for research, letters to foreign municipalities, and organizations for me to get a few answers to the multitude of questions that I have lived with for years. The settling effect of finally getting some answers has created a calm pause, a form of relief.

## SUMMARY

Now I have a better understanding about how and why my father and mother were unable to be present at times, were unable to explain all the grief, fears, and atrocities they experienced, and how each one of their families were torn apart. Separation from family, escaping their country of origin, losses of their families, were so horrendous, that what mattered for them was their desire to brave life head on. The losses they experienced were like a theft; lives were taken from their past and their future generations to come. They were unable to talk about all that happened and kept secrets from me and my siblings or anyone else for that matter. Not only was it an awful time, but also many would not have either comprehended it. They would question if my parents might have been exaggerating their story about what they had gone through. But yet, my parents, with all their diligence, were able to come to grips and handle a family here in America the best way they could. They also lived the best way they knew how.

This has been an exciting development to write down the many various experiences and thoughts I have been able to recollect. I have come to appreciate writing and have so much respect for the written word through this process. Having had the experience of growing up with parents that came from another country, who endured a horrific past and yet were able to adjust to a new way of life in the United States of America, I am optimistic that some of you may have gained some insight about the Holocaust and how a 2G person was affected by such horrific history.

It has been established through several studies that offspring whose parents experienced the Holocaust can be rather wounded by their parents' experiences. Parents' trauma has an effect upon their offspring and affects genes and the way they express themselves. Trauma can be passed down to children through these genes and thus these inherited family patterns can persist. The biological component that affects the gene makeup can be observed over numerous generations. The study of this hereditary science is called Epigenetics.

It definitely was not easy for either one of my parents to learn a new language and culture, after each one of them were forced to flee their country of origin and become a refugee in America. This tome is a testament to their unfailing ways and spirit to not give up and to go on living despite the obstacles and challenges they endured. Through them and despite them, I have been able to appreciate more of what life has been about and the many challenges that life can offer.

As a youth, of course, I had absolutely no knowledge until I was much, much older of what they went through, and had no comprehension of the challenges that they had to deal with head on before arriving to and landing in America, The Land of Golden Opportunity.

I have much compassion, understanding and sadness with the various situations my father and mother had to deal with, the things they wanted to achieve once they arrived in the United States. They wanted to be free from prejudice, live in a safe environment, be left alone to do whatever they wanted and live like anyone else with the opportunities to achieve a life of freedom and victory. There is a feeling that I hold on to regarding how important it is to respect this country and to have the appreciation of what one can achieve if one has the fortitude and willingness to go beyond what is presented to them. My parents were able to survive in American society, this melting pot they call it. Not only then, but also today, so many people want to reach for the liberties that this country cherishes and possesses. America became a place for my refugee parents to turn to be free from the life they left. From what they brought with them, their integrity, I became a person that learned to apply myself and succeed through most any obstacle. Even though there were times that were rather difficult for me to go through as a child and adolescent, my experiences made me a stronger and appreciative person.

The America that I am so familiar with gave my father and mother the ideal to succeed, achieve, and nurture a fresh new life for themselves. It gave them the promise of liberty and hopefully some happiness and peace in each of their lives. They became Americanized the best way they could and were able to gain their economic mobility that is so prevalent for refugees when they arrive to this county, if they work hard enough. And work hard they both did. That did not mean they had to abandon their unique culture that they came from while they brought me up. They brought with them much to this country in the forms of exceptional values of integrity, and class that were passed down to my siblings and me. Through these writings, I have been given the chance to be able to remember and document some significant ideas, episodes, examples and information that furnished my life up until today; how they modeled for me how important it is to work hard, be honest and appreciate the land we live in, to help others and to become and continue to be a respectable human being.

Reminiscing on what I have achieved to this point in my life and what has occurred all through my rearing and beyond, an insight has been given me in what it takes in having endurance, the achievement and longing to create, curiosity and having the best life possible. To keep doing the things necessary to reach one's goals takes a while, and a mind-set of patience and resilience. It was not always easy, but once I was able to get over some major hurdles of what I was experiencing, it became so much easier to continue many of life's experiences.

Encouragement that I have received from friends, educators, and family has given me the impetus to carry on with my writing. When I have felt I could not go on or I had nothing more to add to my writing, I got the necessary kudos, respect, and encouragement to tallyho further. All the silence needed to be broken. What was not being said was as powerful as what was being said. The story needed to be told after all the silence.

Even though this is my history, not until now have I been able to put pen to paper and write down what occurred or what I believe has occurred.

# APPENDIX

Ellen Kotlow from the USC Shoah Foundation Institute for Visual History and Education, conducted an interview of my mother on October 30, 1996, in Albany, New York. Camera was by Henry Shaburn. This is a transcript of the interview my mother gave.

I was born Ruth Markus on June 17, 1910, I am 86 years old at the time of this interview. I married Henry Bischofsheimer, who had just come from Dachau. Five years after he died, I remarried. I am from Neutomischel, a province of Posen (Posnan), the country Germany. I was born German. In 1919 the area became Polish overnight and the town was called Nowy Tomischel.

My early childhood- I came from a very sheltered home. My father and grandfather were in the hop business. We extracted the lupulin of the hop and shipped it all over the world. The town had everything but a library. Our factory was in the back of our house. I didn't play with other children, but I had lots of cousins and aunts to play with. I had one special friend who played with me until I was fourteen, a pastor's daughter, Dorothea who was Protestant, my only friend who became a Diakonin, a nun. I never heard what happened to her. We had our own synagogue in the town comprising of ten to twelve families, having very few children and a few older single women in the shul. (Synagogue) I brought to the single women shalach manos, (Purim baskets of food) but I was afraid, because they had Parkinson's and it scared me.

My mother and father lived in our huge home downstairs with our staff, a man who took care of the horses, a factotum who took care of everything. Grandfather Aaron lived upstairs. We had horses and wagons, but no cars. In 1914, the German authority took away our horses. Young people were being taken away. The hop business was lost by the war. Our horses, wagons and everything was gone. Everyone lived from what they had saved. This was the time going into the war. My father was in the war. They took my father away to a faraway Russian town. In 1919 there was a plague, and my father succumbed to lung disease and died in Hotel Adlon in Berlin. Mother got a card from the German government that said, "Why didn't you pick up the corpse?" She had to go to Berlin and the special police assisted and he was buried in Wiessensee, which is a Jewish cemetery in Berlin. I wish she could've remarried, because she was so young, but in those days right after the war, she was just in her early thirties.

From then on times became different! The Germans shot Grandfather Aaron. He couldn't walk fast enough, because he was too old and became blind. We were very well to-do, I never had a penny of my own, money was not given to me, and I never learned about money. I was taught that it was not nice to talk about it. I had a very large dowry of money given to me that came from the bank. The Germans confiscated the money. I know because I wrote about it. When I came to America, nobody could tell me what actually happened to the money.

When I was twelve years old I went to a private school that was very anti-Semitic. When I took French and was asked to translate, "*Ich bin gekommen zu Schule,*" (I came to school.) I was told, "You are not in the ghetto, speak German." In those days it did not matter; I kept my mouth shut. I went to a Lyceum in Poland.

My mother was five feet, six inches tall like my father. I was very thin and I am very tall like my father or like her brothers. She had dark blond hair; she was so white and never tanned. The non-Jews loved her. My mother's uncle Louie was very fond of my mother. She belonged to the school board, hospital board and to an afternoon group with all Aryan women. She was the only Jew.

My brother was born in 1918 and he was a cutie. There was one problem; he was born too late. I liked and played with dolls; but he was different from my dolls and it scared me. I would sit very stiffly and hold him. When he became older, he would break things and take things, he was a boy, just like kids nowadays. In his teen years, he could not go to school; he was a Jew. My mother didn't want him to sit in the house reading and doing nothing. He learned the leather business, making belts and handbags. He was good with his hands, and he seemed to like it. It's the last time that I know of that. While I was in Breslau (Wroclaw), my brother stayed home with mother. Her father, an invalid with gout who was blind lived with her downstairs. The Germans came. He was very thin. My brother was fed tuberculi in Warsaw and he died. My mother had to leave the house with everything in it and go on the Death March. Grandfather Moses, my mother's father was president of his Jewish community, lived in Pomerania. Grandfather Aaron was the president of our Jewish community.

When I was young there was anti-Semitism in our small town. We never went outside unless we had to go to the store, doctor or dentist. Everything was done in the back of the house, between the factory and our house. I played in the back, playing in the sandbox, and read. Nobody could see me there.

I attended a private school, Lyceum Schule, and then a Ditsayon, private high school for girls. I didn't belong to any organization or school activities. I was a Jew. There were Christmas plays and I had a beautiful voice. In the town where we lived, they wanted me to sing. Grandfather Aaron said, *"Keine Jüdische Mädchen singen."* "No Jewish girl sings Christmas songs." My mother was pleased they selected me to sing in the background.

Goals- As a young person I had no goals as they have here in America. I lived from day to day and loved it. I had my books, music and played piano, went in the woods and brought home little plants to take care of. I didn't know any better. I wasn't interested in cooking and taking care of the house. I was happy, and I didn't know you have to have this or you have to have that, like my children.

My life began to change when I was in Breslau, a very old city. When I went to the seminary, a small school for small children, they only allowed two Jews in their class. We didn't like each other, but I knew there was another Jewish girl. I didn't care for it; I just went through it. I lived with a Jewish lady. I had my own room. I didn't have a friend to my name. I didn't know I needed one; this was 1918-1920. We were all German at that time. Then in 1920 we were not! I was a new Polish person.

My mother did not want me in Poland. When I was home she didn't know what to do with me. She wrote a letter to Uncle Bernard Casparias, who was the brother of my grandfather. He had given the city of Berlin either money or land, where they erected three buildings. One was a quarantine area for new children, another house was just for small babies and their mothers, and another house was like a kindergarten where the children slept. The buildings had lots of land and trees; it was a beautiful place. Uncle Bernard, said, "Oh sure, we are looking for people." The house with the babies was filled; the second house with children who were three to five years in age needed people. Send her over." This was around 1929-1930. I had to go to Warsaw and got my passport. Already things were in the air. I wasn't called a Jid (*Jude*), but Mosaisch. I felt like below anything, it was the first time I felt like I'm not like other people. I loved it at the children's home, called Jüdisches Kinderheim. The director was Dr. Morgenstern; there was Dr. Mendelson, and lots of nurses. One morning in the winter all the children were dead; there was ultra violet light, and we had to be with them. The door opens, the year is 1933, in came the Nazis with their boots up to here with their salute.

They said, "What are you doing here?"

I said, "Come again?"

They said, "Bist *du di Juden*, Ruth Markus?" Are you the Jew Ruth Markus?

I said, "Yes."

They said, "What are you doing here?"

I said, "I'm working here."

They said, "You do not work here, you are a Polack."

I said, "I have my papers upstairs that I can show you."

They said, "You are now in the New German Reich. You're a Polack. You leave this country in twenty-four hours or you go to jail."

My heart sank. That was in the morning. I had to get a *Visum*, (visa), by 3:00 in the afternoon. I had to pack all my books, my lute, my discs, and everything. I was young and I had all those things. I had some friends who helped put me on the train Alexander Platz. I then went home. These were the happy times for me before I was thrown out of Germany.

The home where I worked was gorgeous. It was a stucco place for the babies. A pretty fence surrounded the building; there was a veranda where the babies were in movable baskets, where they could get sunshine. There were lots of nurses, and there were the mothers of the newborn babies who usually had no husbands. Babies were left there when people had to go away for a funeral or wedding; it was like a hotel. These mothers were obligated to breast feed their babies, and help with the laundry and kitchen. They did this for several years and when their babies grew up, what were they to do then? Another house was built to accommodate. In the upper part was the big kindergarten solarium, where there was sunshine, where the children would run around naked. In Europe naked children are at the beaches. There was a bath area, and examination rooms when the doctors came. This was all on the second floor. Below that, the first floor had a library, no kitchen, and dining room for the children. The food was brought in from the old home where the babies were.

The city of Berlin made them build a quarantine area. If new babies came, they might have been ill, they would live there for six weeks before they were put with the other children. They were all dressed alike with shorts and a t-shirt. All the babies and staff were Jewish. I wasn't crazy about some of the staff, but some were very nice. We had children who were there from people who went to America for a talk or something, scientists who had to go somewhere for the summer. I started in the quarantine; and nobody was there, so I was able to get accustomed to this work. I stayed there half a year, and then went on as a kindergarten teacher to the next house. It was very interesting and a good time. It was in Niederschönhausen, a suburb of Berlin. I could take the tram for traveling.

I remember some of the other teachers, Miss Lapidas, who never talked to anybody but knitted neckties for her boyfriend, there was one who was very short and anytime she had the time she would read. The Jews in those days kept to themselves. They were not people who needed outsiders. I didn't know that I was a non-German. I didn't think; if I would have thought, it might have been better. Neutomischel, which became Nowy Tomischel, is 13 miles from Germany.

I'm musical. One evening I came from a recorder society; a recorder is a wooden flute. We played medieval music. I wasn't supposed to be there anymore because I was a *Jude*. (Jew) I could walk from the society home. Six or seven were supposed to be there, we usually had less, and some were very nice. I made the mistake of walking home and playing my recorder. The fences where I lived were all concrete, beautifully done, like Europe. Two youths jumped from the other side of me and I didn't know anything because I was playing the recorder and didn't hold it tight enough, they took my flute and hit me over the head that broke the front part of the flute off. They were lying there like a cat lies in front of mouse hole; they waited for me. The youths knew I was a Jew. Two houses from the incident was the Jewish baby home. I still have a hole in my skull, and I was afraid to go to a doctor, because then they would have forbid me to go to the society. When I came to America, I had trouble with my equilibrium and the doctor sent me to Albany medical College to be examined. They gave me a two-hour examination and couldn't find anything. I just have a good ole head!

I traveled, and went skiing, using wooden skis, I would iron the bottom of them every morning, to Liepnitz, which is between Switzerland and Poland, a mountainous range. I also went to the Baltic Sea, for a week for my vacation which isn't far from where I was born, then I went home two or three times.

I had no feeling of what was to occur. We all thought there were some nuts. We didn't give it much attention to it, till about a month before I was thrown out. There was danger! I also belonged to a college organization against Nazism; they might have known. When I came home, I was moping around, and my mother didn't like it. She said, "You have to do something. You are 25 years old now and you're sitting around the house reading!" I didn't like cooking or cleaning and we had maids. A friend of her, Jews, had a ham factory; they made canned hams for America. "It's funny, isn't it?" they had a little boy who was almost a year old. That was near Bromberg, a well-known city. They called my mother. We had a telephone then. Would I be willing to come and take care of him for a short time? I wasn't willing, but my mother said yes, I went there. He was the cutest little thing. He didn't speak yet. Nobody had taken care of him in a way a mother would have. He was the cutest little boy, very bright. I had my work cut out and stayed two years. His name was Yeggy, which means George. I forgot their last name.

I got a call from my mother that she has just heard that Uncle Louie died in America and the lawyers want to see her. Could I come and take care of the two grandfathers? "If you want me to, I come," I said. I went, mother went and her father had a stroke. Dr. Boudette, who delivered me, said, "Ruth, don't call her back, this is the end." He was eighty-four years, there's nothing we can do, and he died. There was the chevra kadisha, the Jewish burial society that every Jewish community has. There are twelve men and four women. The women are the ones who wash the body. The men are the ones who take care of the cemetery. I went through that and felt terrible.

When she came back, she said, "Ruth, everything is all right. America is wonderful. *Es ist so ein grosses Land.*" (Such a big land.) "Everybody smiles and people don't work, they just have money."

She went from the upper circle, they all had money. The year was nineteen thirty-five. Uncle Louie Jacobson was her father's brother. Uncle Louie left my mother six thousand dollars, which in those days is like sixty thousand now.

She said, "Ruth, now we are going to America. It's wonderful; we are going to have something to live for. You go first and see something."

"Mutte, how can I go? I don't know anybody. What shall I do there? I'm happy here."

She said, "No, you're going."

She went to Warsaw and paid under the table a large amount to get my *Visum*, (visa) and I left. I see myself standing on the peron, (platform to wait for a train) in the station, the train is moving, and mother stands there. I don't want to think about it. I went via Gdansk via Danzig, across Norway and Sweden.

We landed in Halifax. All I was allowed to take was twenty-five dollars or one hundred Reichsmark. I took my doll along; I don't know why, two linen large napkins. When each family inherits their napkins, each one puts their monogram on each corner. My forefathers in the eighteen hundreds were linen weavers. Slowly I forgot the bitterness. Nobody talked to me on the trip. Everybody was seasick but five nuns and me. I never had any food like that because where I come from a kosher household. I never saw cantaloupe and I never drank orange juice. It was a wonder to me. Mother's sister with her husband left Stettin, Germany overnight around the time of Kristallnacht, where the Nazis broke and ruined everything. I had relatives I was going to see when I arrived in the United States. I lived with them, paid for my stay from Uncle Louie's money to help them. Uncle Herman who was a fine man became an elevator operator. He died.

From Halifax, in two days we were in New York. The visa people had to be there. They got me from the boat and I stayed with them. I didn't like it too well. They were old. I still thought it's just a short while and Mutti, my mother will come. I didn't understand it. I was very inexperienced with other people. I never had a boyfriend. I don't know what happened to my girlfriend Dorothea. I went to the Jewish agency in Manhattan in New York City, where people who need help go. There was no help for us, no help for refugees. Still, I was just a visitor. I got a call from Rabbi Wise's granddaughter; they needed somebody for their two children. They lived near Central Park and 5th Avenue and 60$^{th}$ Street. This was 1937 in United States. The children were such mean little kids. They would run across 5$^{th}$ Avenue away from me, and would not listen to me. They would make fun of my very German accent. Rabbi Wise came visiting; he was darling. I wish his daughter had been a darling. It hurt me so, because if they get killed, I would be responsible, so I left. There was no agency that would give you the time of day. Rosh Hashanah came. I wanted to go to temple, so I walked at least two blocks to the temple on East 64 or 68 Street, I don't remember any more, and they didn't let me in because I hadn't paid. I walked home and slept on the couch. I took a job near New Rochelle advertised in the newspaper. There was a little girl I watched whom I liked very much.

I had tickets for the evening to listen to Mrs. Roosevelt talk at Hunter College, but I was brought up that no Jewish girl at night walks alone. You always have somebody with you. Siegfried whom I knew from Germany was now working in a store, called me to tell me that he cannot come because he is going out to meet somebody on the boat and he had to be there. He was awfully sorry and sending the man who lived near him, someone who is also Jewish, a good man, don't worry. I had no transportation; he didn't either. I took the bus to 49 Street and then we walked. There he was, he didn't even doff his hat. I didn't like him and he didn't like me. He wouldn't even spend thirty cents to get a hotdog and an orange juice. I thought that's terrible. He was from Munich, a refugee. That was in November. I said forget about this. I told Siegfried what a jerk he was.

Somebody came up and said, "There's a man out there and wants to talk to you."

I said, "I don't know any man and I don't want to talk to him."

He said, "He insists he knows you."

So, I got curious, that maybe he would be from my hometown. No, it was Henry! He had just bought an old Chevrolet. You should have seen that car.

He said, "Wouldn't you like to take a drive with me?"

I said, "I don't know you sir. You were so awful that night I went to Hunter College; I don't want to see you anymore."

He said, "Well, I was that way because I don't want any…"

He was from the South and I was from the North. The Jews hated each other. You were supposed to be either Bavarian or the other part, Prussian. This afternoon I'm off, come back again, I'm busy now, and then maybe I take a ride. I took a ride and I married him a year later. He just didn't want me to like him. He told me how terrible it was for him to become human again; that he was in Dachau and he didn't want to talk about it. In those days I didn't even know what Dachau was, because we didn't know it. Franklin D. Roosevelt was a very nice man, but when it comes to Jews he really forgot what's what. The American public was not notified. We got married downtown in New York City. We lived in an apartment of one room. My bathroom now is bigger than that room was. And we were not happy. We were worried about our people. We were worried about what we should do. What we went through there was nobody in those days to help us, nobody. What we didn't do ourselves, and then nothing was done.

I went to evening school to improve my English that nobody could understand, because I learned Ivanhoe and Shakespeare and they didn't speak Shakespeare in New York City. There was a very nice small Italian teacher whom I fell in love with. When I lived in New York, I couldn't do anything. I was applying for first papers. I wanted to go to Canada to leave the country, but Canada closed its borders, they had an infantile paralysis outbreak. So, I had to go to Cuba.

Everybody said, "My god, you go to Cuba, it's terrible. Nobody speaks German there."

I said, "I don't want to speak German."

They said, "There's nobody from home."

The Paseo del Prado, a beautiful street in Havana with trees over hanging the benches, was full of refugees waiting for their quota number. All you could hear was Viennese, German, Thüringen, Munich, and all these dialects. I didn't intend to sit on the Paseo del Prado and cry and think of the people I left, so I lived with natives. I spent my time at the beach. This was around nineteen thirty-eight- nineteen thirty-nine. I was 28 or 29. This was before New York, before I got married.

I didn't know I was good looking then, because I was brought up not to look in the mirror. All these young men were after me; I disliked it. I didn't know what to do. I have never dated and I have never been embraced but by my uncle who would give me a peck on the cheek. I had no idea, so I stayed away from them. I was there almost two years when my number came up. I met many European people there who impressed me, people with degrees, Einstein's, people who were nothing, just men and wives. All I could hear was crying. I didn't intend to do that. I didn't believe in that, even if it all ended tomorrow. I went back to New York and applied for my citizenship. That's when I married Henry. I got my citizenship. I went to school and learned about the Senate, Washington, which is completely untrue, if you ask me. I learned about the government and I could sing the national Anthem, three verses, but don't ask me now, I don't know anymore. I became a citizen. I had to go to New York. In those days we lived in Nassau, New York. While Henry and I were married, we went to Horne & Hardart, a famous cafeteria where you would put a dime or five cents in the machine, open a little door and there was your food. I loved chicken salad, because I had never had it in my life in Europe, kosher kitchen, you know! I almost died.

The mayonnaise, something went wrong. We didn't go to a doctor; we didn't have the money. Henry worked at Leeds Importers on Fourteen Street. He couldn't miss a day. His salary was six dollars a week. When he married me, they gave him a dollar special, so he had seven dollars a week. We lived from that.

Early years living in New York City, I had contact with my mother; letters came opened and stamped "Geoffnet," by the Nazis. She was in the ghetto now in Warsaw. My brother was with my mother in the Warsaw ghetto, too. She wrote that he's not feeling well, coughing a lot, that she had lots of friends there naturally, and that everything would be all right. That's what they thought. The world doesn't believe us. She wrote as though she would see me tomorrow. The card said that they are all well, that Horst is sick; naturally, they fed him tuberculi. He was so thin you could see his ribs. That was before. Then- Nothing. Then the Red Cross told me what happened. I had no contact with my mother after I got a card from Warsaw. I sent money, stupidly, which the Germans I'm sure took. Then it all stopped. I had no contact with my mother after I got a card from Warsaw. Whether she died in the ghetto uprising, I don't know. The Swiss Red Cross let us know that they both were there.

The Germans were so wonderful, they wrote everything down, even the negative things. There were the names. My grandfather Aaron wasn't even mentioned, when they shot him down at the death march. My husband Henry got news what happened to his family. We were devastated.

I was pregnant with Pat. Henry didn't want any children, no more Jewish children, but I liked babies.

When she was born, I was so pleased. I don't know what's the matter with me. I couldn't cry at my second husband's burial, but I cry today! We didn't know what to call her. We knew Henry had a grandmother who passed away; Carolyn, so we gave her that name and I wanted to let the world know that she comes from a noble family, so I named her Patricia, only to find out that Patricia is a typical Irish name here. Boy, I'm glad I don't have to go through this again.

Henry came from Dachau Concentration camp. He didn't confide in me but he confided in a friend of my children, Mr. Louis Ismay, who works at the Schenectady Museum. After Henry died, Lou said, come to me, come here, and hugged me and told me what they made him do. They made them make a circle and they put a gay person or a gypsy, even less than a Jew, they had to beat him to death. I thought I could make Henry alive, I never could. At his funeral the rabbi said, "Now he's happy." They also made him dig ditches one day and open the ditches another day and if the ditch was not done by five o'clock; they made him stand overnight in the cold water. Henry's legs were just one varicose vein after another. I thought I could help him. Forget it.

Life in America- After two and in a half years I had a little boy, over six foot today, named Jamie. I didn't want to call him Jacob, after grandfather who already died, because it's too German. I called him James, I'm sorry now. Six years after Pat was born, I had Rosalie. The children were so sweet. My gynecologist, Dr. Klinger, I adored. I had fibroid troubles.

Dr. Klinger always said, "How's my Prussian girl?" when he saw me.

He said, "You haven't got fibroid troubles, you are pregnant."

I said, "I cannot be pregnant, I'm too old," I was forty-four.

He said, "Well you are!"

He had given me medication for female trouble. Don't buy anything, that child might never be human when I deliver it. He was supposed to be born in August. In March I took a photography course during my spring vacation in the old East Greenbush High School. It was stuffy in the room. I opened the window. I said, "What the hell is the matter with me?" I'm urinating in a classroom, I didn't urinate, and I had a miscarriage. I taught in East Greenbush and Castleton in those days. They sent for an ambulance and I gave my ring that my daughter has now to the young woman I had with me. You weren't allowed to take anything to the hospital, and I thought I would die. I had cramps and then at midnight I lost two little boys, twins, four and one half months old that were identical. In two days I was home. We had no money. He said I have to make a DNC on you, which was the law and I don't want you to lose your money, Memorial Day weekend you don't teach, come then. He had an Irish nurse whom I loved and they put me on the table. Her Irish screaming and his Austrian screaming, I was still pregnant! I didn't believe it. There were two little boys whom I lost; I didn't believe it. He said, "Yes, you are, I can feel it." He was five months old. He said, "Ruth, don't buy anything for this child, this is not a normal business. I was put on a diet, cottage cheese, hard rolls, tea and oatmeal. He was born just marvelous, wonderful; he's my baby, six foot something, ski instructor; the healthiest baby you ever wanted to see. Dr. Kinger made me get a hysterectomy. He said, "It's enough. We have one Jewish mother not enough."

I had lots of friends. There was a lady, Ethel Angela Bingham when we lived in Nassau, New York, who was a wonderful person. She married her husband on his deathbed. She was from New York. She lived all alone in Nassau, Seven Oaks, very English, very British and she took care of me and she saw the baby; Pat was her baby. She made me an American. She taught me how to eat squash, American vegetables, which I never would have eaten. Carrots and onions yes, but not those things. She was the head of the Red Cross in Rennselaer County. Ethel Angela took me along all over and introduced me and I got lots of friends. They did not know I existed. She had a cousin, Miss Bradley, who lived with her who fell in love with Pat as a baby. They were true Americans, wonderful, dead now, wonderful people. They were not Jews, but they helped me any bit. They stood up for me when I became a citizen, they told Henry he should be more careful with me, I'm a woman. Henry was very demanding. He was an artist too. He took a class from Dr. Ackerman from Rennselaer who taught an art class in adult education. He enjoyed it so. When he was so disturbed, he painted a beautiful picture and when he was finished, he would tear it up. He was just hurt. That's what the Germans did to him.

Some things I like to add. I didn't grow up in Poland. In Germany, my mother stayed with a family. In my vacation time I would go to grandfather and her younger sister and enjoy it there. We did not visit each other but we were very nice to each other. We stayed by ourselves. I loved books, making things, but it was a sheltered affair. I was happy and I didn't miss anything.

There are messages to leave for my children and grandchildren; there are so many. First, don't believe anything somebody tells you, because there are two to three sides to every story, maybe even more. Second, take care of each other. You are all you have of your own family. Third, everybody says, "Don't you love him, don't you love her?" Love is something completely different. When a woman falls in love, it is something out of her body, something wonderful, but you have to find out whether the person is for you. Marriage is great, if you can be the right person for the other. If you are just a woman and a man, then it is just sex, it's nothing, and there has to be more. You have to have hope and unification. You also have to make allowances for other people. It is not going to be the same as in the beginning; it is quite different later on.

For more information: http://sfi.usc.edu

Memoir of a 2G

# ACKNOWLEDGMENTS

Thanks to the following people that without their encouragement to continue writing and helping me on my passage of writing this memoir, I might not have wanted to go on. I am grateful to friends who had the fortitude and willingness to read parts or all of my manuscript and made their constructive evaluations: Sterling Vinson, Michlean Amir, Barbara Kosta, Ephraim Zimmerman, Michaela Willi Hooper, Adena Bank Lees, Rosario Russell Ruggiero, Zachary Spahr, Volker R. Berghahn Joel Nathan, Donna Mae Gildart, Jerry D. Isaacs, and United States Holocaust Memorial Museum. Additional thanks go to the Writers' Motivational Workshop.

Thanks go to my parents, Henry and Ruth, for without them, my story would not have been told.

I Patricia C Bischof gratefully acknowledge the USC Shoah Foundation for allowing me to use transcript of the following: Ruth Renzema, October 30, 1996. For more information: http://sfi.usc.edu

Memoir of a 2G

# ABOUT THE AUTHOR

Patricia Bischof divides her time with Tucson, Arizona, and Manhattan, New York. Her interests and hobbies include genealogy, antiquing, traveling, music, vintage women's accessories and art. She received her BA from Prescott College in Arizona.

Made in the USA
San Bernardino, CA
16 January 2019